how to plant your allotment

how to plant your allotment

Caroline Foley

NH
NEW
HOLLAND

First published in 2007 by New Holland Publishers (UK) Ltd
London · Cape Town · Sydney · Auckland

Garfield House, 86–88 Edgware Road, London W2 2EA, United Kingdom
www.newhollandpublishers.com

80 McKenzie Street, Cape Town 8001, South Africa
Level 1, Unit 4, 14 Aquatic Drive, Frenchs Forest, NSW 2086, Australia
218 Lake Road, Northcote, Auckland, New Zealand

ISBN 978 184537 616 1

Senior Editor: Clare Sayer
Production: Hazel Kirkman
Design: Casebourne Rose Design Associates
Allotment plans: Caroline Foley
Techniques diagrams: Coral Mula
Cover photographs: Sue Rose
Editorial Direction: Rosemary Wilkinson

10 9 8 7 6 5 4 3 2 1

Reproduction by Modern Age Repro, Hong Kong
Printed and bound in India by Replika Press Pvt. Ltd.

CONTENTS

INTRODUCTION

This book aims to divulge a few golden tips of the trade.

The idea struck me when I came across a modest volume entitled *The Intensive Culture of Vegetables on the French System – with a Concise Monthly Calendar of Operations by P. Aquatius , formerly a gardener to A. J. Molynoux Esq.* Writing in 1913, M. Aquatius advocates the techniques used by the French smallholders selling their produce at Les Halles in Paris. The book is a guide to running a market garden as efficiently and economically as a Swiss clock. I thought that, though our aims and standards are less exacting than those of professional growers, it might be useful to take a glimpse at their way of doing things.

The first essential, says Monsieur Aquatius, is a perfect knowledge of the life cycle and the needs of each plant. 'Crops succeed one another every six weeks; and, after each, the cultivator finds his soil as productive and workable as before.' 'Everything is weighted, calculated, timed and checked; every crop has a cycle of growth to follow and it must work as a piece of ingenious mechanism for the others that succeed it.'

I concluded that successful streamlining comes from planning ahead and lateral thinking. If, for example, you are designing an allotment plot from scratch, making the beds a uniform size with cloches tailored to fit them precisely gives you maximum flexibility for minimum effort later on. With this arrangement, you can start an efficient system of 'strip cropping'.

The idea is to have parallel beds of equal width with enough cloches of the right size to fit every other row. As one crop no longer needs them, they are moved with minimum effort to the adjacent row for a new crop that does. So, for example, hardy peas are cloched through winter. By early summer they prefer to be out in the open air and the cloches are moved over to the parallel bed for young outdoor cucumbers or melons that will relish the heat. By autumn these are harvested and the cloches are moved back to the first bed for winter cabbage and spring greens in the New Year.

One of the many checklists in this book shows the minimum temperatures that individual vegetables need to get into active growth. As we all know, the less time plants spend idle as sitting ducks for pests the better. The aim should always be to grow plants strongly, quickly and unchecked. By planting at the optimum time you are falling into step with nature – the best ally you can have.

The standard way of planting is in military rows or drills. Yet straight rows were originally designed for the horse-drawn plough and the seed drill, not for the plot holder and his hoe. If you have narrow beds, do you need rows? By adding the recommended planting and row distances together and halving the total, you have the measurement for an equidistant pattern. By planting so there are no gaps, you can provide continuous leaf cover with the benefit that it will shade out weeds. If there is no overlap between plants, they won't be competing with each other so each can grow to its full potential.

If, on the other hand, you want 'baby veg' you can, with certain vegetables, arrange this by closer spacing. Onion growers have always known that they can get small onions by planting close and big ones with wider spacing without affecting the quality. Trials by the National Vegetable Research Station (see pages 84–86) show that the spacing of leeks can be cut down by as much as ten times for 'mini' leeks. You might decide to grow some big and some small for different occasions and dishes.

Trials also showed that outdoor bush tomatoes planted at half the recommended distance produced more in the early part of the season (when tomatoes are expensive) and less at the end (when there is a glut).

The skilled gardener can make even more use of the space by 'interplanting', 'underplanting' and 'catch cropping'. The principle is to keep a few beds in tip-top condition for intensive growing. This saves having to keep the entire plot up to scratch. Between the slow growers like Brussels sprouts, you can 'catch crop' by planting quick growers like spring onions or radishes in between. They will be harvested long before the sprouts need the extra space. Equally you can 'underplant' tall plants like sweetcorn with short ones like lettuce. Lettuce will enjoy the sun in spring and the shade provided by corn in summer. This is, in other words, an ideal partnership. 'Interplanting' can combine narrow with wide – the slim leaves of the onion family between the broad leaves of cabbage or cauliflower.

The plans in Chapter 5 are thumbnail sketches aimed to try out ideas on different themes. They are not to be taken too literally. The Big Family Plot aims to provide as much produce as possible all year round. There is always more coming up in the cold frames ready to be planted as soon as there is a gap. The varieties chosen are the nation's tried and tested favourites.

The High-speed Plot is a caricature sketch of a plot for people in a hurry. A growing-season only plot, it is planned for minimum maintenance right down to buying the plants as 'plugs'. Even the salads are purchased on pre-sown mats. Most of the plants have the RHS Award of Garden Merit – a good choice as they are guaranteed to be good growers and generally trouble free.

The Italian and Heritage Plots are exercises in locating particular types of plants. They proved to be an enjoyable challenge as there are many wonderful old and new Italian varieties of vegetables, as well as a wide choice of 19th-century varieties for the Heritage Plot. These have not been bettered or replaced by modern seed breeders, nor hidden away in heritage seed libraries, but are up there in the mainstream catalogues. In case these varieties weren't as pest-resistant as the latest cultivars, the Heritage Plot is exemplary in bio-diversity.

In The Ornamental Plot, it wasn't too hard to grade the vegetables from the hot end of the colour spectrum through to cool blues and purples. It turned out to be a rather gorgeous affair with 'Scarlet Emperor' runner beans and 'Crystal Lemon' cucumbers at one end and 'Blue Lake' French beans and 'Violette de Provençe' artichokes at the other.

For The Oriental Plot the tender vegetables are grown in a polytunnel. The point of this plot is to see which oriental vegetables can be usefully and easily grown outside in the British climate. Sticking to UK seed catalogues, I was able to find many suitable new varieties. Most spring up without any

problem and are brilliant in the winter months, particularly for the 'hungry gap' for greens and cut-and-come-again salad leaves.

The trickiest of all was The Caribbean Plot. The challenge was to find out whether it is possible to grow semi-tropical produce in a temperate climate outside of a heated greenhouse. While we can probably never grow a mango, we can – with a little luck and skill – grow chillies and even okra outside on the allotment in most parts of Britain.

Monsieur Aquatius wisely points out that you will undoubtedly find that the vegetables you are best at growing will be the ones that grow best for you. He is, of course, absolutely right. Yet my hope is that this book will build up your confidence and help to increase your repertoire of skills. Then you might play around a little with the old rules, take small risks, push the boundaries out and get ever more pleasure and satisfaction from your plot.

CHAPTER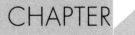

the site

This chapter explores the differences between allotment sites – council-owned, temporary, statutory, private, self- and council-managed. It looks at the pros and cons so that prospective allotmenteers can make an informed choice regarding which site will be best for them. It considers the history, the legal rights, different attitudes and what to expect in terms of facilities – as well as what might be expected of you.

HISTORY AND BACKGROUND

Although allotment numbers have dwindled to half what they were during the Second World War, there still remains an allotment holder in every sixteenth house across England and Wales. There are some 330,000 plots, mostly along railway sidings, but also tucked away behind housing estates and in other small pockets of land on the outskirts of towns.

Allotments originally sprung from the need to relieve the plight of the 'labouring poor'. With the advent of the Industrial Revolution in the 18th century, unemployment was sweeping through the countryside. The hardships were made worse by the Enclosure Acts which effectively removed the 'common land' where villagers could grow produce and keep livestock.

The term 'labouring poor' was finally deleted in the Land Facilities Settlement Act of 1919. Everyone was urgently needed to pitch into the war effort, so allotments were then officially opened to all and sundry, rich and poor alike. As a result, in England and Wales an allotment plot is virtually a citizen's right. If there are no allotments in a particular area, any six residents on the electoral role together have the right to demand one and the council must provide. The only exceptions to this are inner London boroughs without spare green space. Rather like votes for women, allotments were bitterly fought for and hard won.

Allotments today

Following a sad decline, there has been a sea change in attitude. Allotments today have risen to become the last word in political

DID YOU KNOW?

Some eight per cent of allotments are privately owned and the allotment holders have few rights. Five per cent are 'temporary' sites on land leased or rented by an allotments authority. The vast majority, 87 per cent of sites, are council-owned 'statutory' allotments that are well protected from closure.

CLOSED SITES

When an allotment site is closed, the allotment authority must give displaced plot holders adequate alternative sites 'suitable for spade cultivation', no further than three-quarters of a mile from the centre of demand. Displaced plot holders are also entitled to compensation for their crops, for any manure they have applied to the land, and up to one year's rent.

correctness. All the buzz words apply to them – 'sustainability', 'environment' and 'community'. They fit in with the push for healthy living, increased exercise, the 'five a day' fruit and vegetables campaign, as well as the organic movement. Gardening reaches across cultures and is also a medically accepted therapy. There are allotments for people in trauma, even for the victims of torture. Quite a few specifically aim to meet the needs of Asian women. A plot of land can provide all sorts of people with a safe environment to meet each other and grow their own food.

An influx of the young and educated has brought new blood and fresh skills – particularly computer skills – to the membership. There is a tangible new energy in the allotment world. And with it comes money from charities willing to help regenerate them.

Statutory allotments

Statutory allotments are owned by councils and can only be sold or used for other purposes when given the consent of the Secretary of State for Transport, Local Government and the Regions. Apart from truly exceptional circumstances (like the building of the Channel Tunnel or the Olympic Village), the council needs to prove that the allotment is 'surplus to requirements' before it can sell it.

good idea

The best way to protect your allotment site from being sold off by the council is to keep it fully occupied and in full use. Generate as much interest in the community as you can.

In the past there have been cases of allotments being allowed to fall into disrepair and being left open to vandalism. This has the natural consequence of the plotholders losing heart and giving up. Then a case has been made that there was no demand and the site has been closed.

This loophole has been sewn up by a select committee report entitled *The Future for Allotments* (1998). It recommended that temporary sites of more than 30 years should become statutory and that local authorities should appoint an allotment officer, provide water and fencing, advertise vacant plots and consult plot holders prior to sale. More importantly, the Government recommended that local authorities should promote allotment sites before selling them. So councils are now required to show that they have advertised any spare plots and that they have consulted the plot holders.

SOME HISTORICAL DATES

1649 Gerald Winstanley and 'The Diggers' camped on former common land in Walton-on-Thames, Surrey. The army was called in to burn their huts and rip out their crops.

1830 The Captain Swing Riots. Large groups of farm workers moved from farm to farm smashing machinery. Most of the ringleaders were deported. In the same year the Act to Amend the Laws for the Relief of the Poor permitted parishes to set aside up to 50 acres of wasteland for allotments.

1887 The Allotments Act. Local Authorities must supply allotments where there is demand.

1908 The Smallholding and Allotments Act. Local authorities are given the power to compulsorily purchase land for allotments, also to sell them if they believe they are surplus to need.

1919 Land Facilities Settlement Act. Reference to the 'labouring poor' is deleted. Allotments are open to all.

1922 Allotments Act. An allotment may not exceed 40 poles and should be used 'wholly or mainly for the production of fruit and vegetables' for the plot holder and his family.

1923 Statutory sites may not be sold without ministerial consent.

1924 Allotments Act. Tenants may keep rabbits and hens. A year's notice to quit is required. Concessions may be made on rent.

FINDING THE RIGHT SITE

To find out about what is available in your area call your local Parish, Town, Borough or District Council. The local library should also have a list of allotment sites in the area. Some councils even have allotment departments.

Councils vary in how much importance they attach to their allotments. The best will be encouraging and welcome newcomers. They may provide literature, run courses for beginners and put on summer shows, open days and entertainments. They will be active in National Allotments' Week in August. Some councils even prepare the land for new members.

See as many sites as possible

Hopefully your plot will become your home from home, your club, the place where you unwind and relax. It's important that you feel comfortable there and will get along with the neighbours. Closeness to home is another crucial factor.

Compare the amenities

Fences, hedges and locked gates at night are essential against vandalism – one of the banes of allotments. Check the watering arrangements. Councils are expected to supply mains water at a convenient distance for plot holders. Many allotments provide sheds. Toilet facilities are becoming less of a rarity. Some sites have a clubhouse for meetings or a trading shed where you can buy gardening goods at more or less trade prices. Others will have tools or machinery for the use of members.

Once you have made your choice, you may have to wait before you get a plot. The availability of plots varies enormously from area to area. Once you are on the waiting list, it is worth befriending the committee or manager. Show them that you are really keen. They will be looking for people who are going to fit in and look after their plots well. They may even be able to fast track you, depending on the rules.

Allotment management

The way in which the allotment is managed can make all the difference to a site. In two-thirds of council sites, Local Authority allotment officers deal with the day-to-day management and any disputes. The remaining third of sites are run by allotment societies who manage the site on a lease scheme.

Twenty-five per cent of sites have a group membership with the National Society of Allotment and Leisure Gardeners (NSALG). Founded in 1930, its main role is to give advice on the preparation of leases and agreements between landlords and plot holders and to assist with interpretations of the law and legal disputes. It produces advice leaflets, covering a range of issues affecting plot holders, and runs a bulk seed scheme.

THE ALLOTMENT COMMITTEE

When choosing an allotment, find out about the committee as they can have a major impact on the site. A good committee may organize lectures, open days, even garden visits. They might get in manure in bulk from local stables or leaves for leafmould from the parks. The more enterprising may have a stall at the local farmer's market to raise the profile. They might have a flower show and an open day. Some have a website with links to other allotments in the area. Keeping a high profile and drawing in the local community is good practice and, from a selfish point of view, a wise precaution against any threats to sell off the site.

THE LEASE

There is no yardstick on rents, except they should be no more than what a tenant can 'reasonably be expected to pay'. Generally, rents are very cheap, no more than a few pounds a week. There are usually concessions for retired allotment holders. When you take on a plot you will probably be asked to sign a lease. Usually the terms will be along the following lines.

◆ You should grow mainly fruit and vegetables on your plot for the use of your family. This is not strictly enforced as a general rule.

◆ You may not sell your produce.

◆ You may not run a business from your plot.

◆ You may not sublet it.

◆ You must keep it in good order.

◆ There may be restrictions on water and bonfires.

ENDING A LEASE

The lease agreement will usually include provision for the tenancy to be ended by either the plot holder or the authority.

If the authority or association wishes to end a tenancy it will need to give the plot holder a year's notice, expiring on or before the 6 April or after the 29 September in any year. However, if the rent is unpaid or the tenant fails to comply with the terms of tenancy, a month's notice is usually sufficient.

◆ You must not cause a nuisance.

◆ There are often guidelines on the use of pesticides and herbicides.

◆ Some allotment sites ban barbed wire.

◆ Some put limits on the size of sheds, greenhouses, polytunnels and other structures.

◆ Trees are usually not allowed.

CHAPTER

2

the
plot

A simple survey can reveal vital information about the soil and the conditions that will affect what you grow and how you grow it. This chapter looks at ways to overcome problems such as strong winds, poor soil and rampant perennial weeds. It explains how to make a basic plan and work towards it step-by-step in the most economic and time-saving fashion.

HOW MUCH SPACE?

The first decision to make is whether to go for a full plot. If you share the view that allotment gardening should be as much about enjoying quality time as about producing food, you may find that a whole plot is more than you really need. Keep in mind that the size of the standard allotment was worked out to be the right size for an 18th- or 19th-century farm labourer to be able to feed his family of six.

Allotment people take pleasure in being individualistic and still talk in poles – a measurement strange to most and only dimly remembered by others from the mists of their schooldays. This is hardly surprising as poles went out of date with the Weights and Measures Act of 1836 and 1837. The same as the perch and rod, a pole is 5.02 m (16 ft 6 in), the length of stick needed by the mediaeval ploughman to reach the leading pair of his team of eight oxen.

The ten-pole allotment, therefore, works out in modern currency at approximately 250 sq m (303 sq yd). A wartime cropping plan recommended by the Royal Horticultural Society allowed six of the ten poles – over half the plot – to be turned over to potatoes. They calculated that this would produce 10 cwt (about 450 kg or 1,000 lbs) each year. That's 1.5 kg (3 lb 3 oz) of potatoes each week for every man, woman and child – a huge amount by today's standards for our small nuclear families.

If you think a whole plot might be too much for your needs and the time you will spend on it, consider taking on a half plot. Some allotments have even smaller 'beginner's plots'. Another idea would be to share a full plot with some friends or neighbours. This gives you the added advantage of having someone to cover for you during holidays and in emergencies.

CHOOSING A PLOT

If you have a choice of plots, spend some time weighing up the pros and cons of each.

Good points

✦ **Facilities** Some plots may have the advantage of a greenhouse or polytunnel that you can purchase or inherit.

✦ **Water** It is a great advantage to be close to a source of water, usually a standpipe.

✦ **Access** Good access by road will mean less barrowing of manure, wood chips and leaves when they are delivered.

✦ **A clear plot** A weed-free plot could save years of work.

✦ **High standard of the other plots** If your neighbours maintain their plots to a reasonable standard you won't suffer from their neglect with their weed seeds blowing in.

✦ **Good soil** Find out about the soil in different parts of the

allotment. Ask the neighbours and see if the plants look healthy. Lush weeds are a sign of good fertile soil, particularly if there are stinging nettles, chickweed and docks among them.

✦ **Shelter** Research shows that wind-free zones can increase productivity by as much as 30 per cent.

✦ **Privacy** If this matters to you, a corner plot might be a good choice.

Bad points

✦ **Weeds** Avoid a plot full of difficult perennial weeds if possible, although you may not have much choice. Plots are

good idea

Find out as much as you can about the site from the neighbours. Gather information and tips. Talk to them about what grows well and what the winter conditions may hold.

usually vacated in a neglected state. If the former tenant has been given notice to leave, it is likely that the plot will have been neglected for over a year. The months pass as warning letters are sent to the former tenant before they are given the statutory notice. Tenants can only be evicted more quickly if they break the rules or fail to pay the rent. If your plot is very weedy, some councils will make an allowance on the rent for the first year, so it is worth asking.

✦ **A windswept site** You will be giving yourself an uphill battle. A current of air is healthy and prevents the build up of pests and disease, but young plants are highly susceptible to cold drying winds. Combined with frost, high winds can kill.

✦ **A frost pocket** An allotment in a frost pocket will be useless for growing produce.

✦ **Overhanging trees** A plot with an overhang of trees should be avoided for reasons of shade, and because the trees will take nutrients and moisture from the soil.

✦ **Poor soil** Really poor soil is unlikely in land that has been cultivated over the years for growing vegetables. However, if the plants (or weeds) look sparse and sickly, or the soil looks waterlogged, do some checks before committing yourself to the plot.

note

Some allotment committees rotavate the land for new tenants. Although it makes the plot look good at the time, it doesn't deal with the perennial weeds which will return with renewed vigour.

THE SURVEY

When you have chosen your plot, start by surveying it to gather information on which to base your decisions about how to divide up the space and what to grow. Arm yourself with a notebook and a pencil if the skies look menacing (ballpoints don't work in the rain).

Measure or pace out your plot and sketch it out roughly to scale in your notebook. Mark in any existing features like a shed, existing paths or trees. Take a reading with a compass or observe the position of the sun and mark in the north with an arrow. Next find out where the prevailing winds are and mark them on your plan.

Visit your plot regularly and observe and make note of anything that strikes you, like frost pockets or damp patches. Mark these into your survey plan. A damp patch might be a good place to site a small pond or put in a raised bed.

If you take photographs you can monitor your progress as you go. It is always fascinating to look back and see how far you have come and how things have changed.

Aspect

The ideal aspect is south facing for all-day sunshine. Most annual vegetables need as much sunshine as a UK summer will provide. They are best planted in rows running north to south so they don't shade each other in summer. If your allotment site is divided into a patchwork of flat rectangles, as they usually are, you should be able to make your rows of vegetables face in any direction.

Slope

A site that has a steep slope is less than ideal for reasons of soil erosion. It can be dealt with by making parallel terraces like a series of steps. The beds should go across rather than up the slope. With vertical channels it will be easy to irrigate from the top.

WINDBREAKS

If you are on a windy site, make a note to put in windbreaks in some form. Living and man-made types are both effective.

You cannot block out the wind with a solid barrier like a wall. The wind will whip over the top, becoming ever more furious and making more turbulence on the far side than it would otherwise have done. The most effective windbreaks filter the wind, breaking its force and calming it.

Suitable materials for windbreaks are shrubs and hedges, both evergreen and deciduous. If conditions are mild and the allotment committee allows it, you could consider an alcoholic country hedge of elderflower, sloe and plums. Lath or wattle fencing, trelliswork, plastic windbreak netting or mesh are also highly effective.

Plantings of Jerusalem artichokes, sunflowers or sweet corn will make a little oasis for vegetables (and perhaps a draft-free sunspot for you) in summer if the wind is not too strong. In Japan they use wind barriers of bamboo. These are just giant grasses with tremendous tensile strength.

A solid windbreak creates turbulence while a permeable one filters the wind and can cut its force by half.

TYPES OF WINDBREAK

✦ **Hedging,** if allowed by the allotment committee, is very effective and looks good but it will take a few years to establish. Hedges take nutrients and water from the soil and need clipping. A loose hedge will take up quite a wide space, about 90 cm (3 ft).

✦ **Lath and wattle fencing** or trellis are excellent and blend into the background. Lath fencing needs gaps in it to work as a windbreak. Trellis can be painted to decorative effect. All have the advantage of being doubly useful as they form a structure for growing climbing vegetables, flowers or fruit as well as acting as a windbreak. Make sure that the posts are dug in good and deep. Once set up, they are trouble free for a few years.

✦ **Fruit trees** trained into espaliers or cordons are both decorative and productive as windbreaks, though they are not suitable for high winds. The construction is cheap and easy compared to any sort of fencing. Often the committees will make an exception to their no-tree rule and allow trained trees on dwarf stock.

✦ **Wire or plastic netting** is highly effective as a windbreak, but something of an eyesore and expensive to buy. To secure it firmly, lay it against sturdy posts and nail the battens over it. It is also useful for protecting young hedges and espaliers until they become established.

HOW TALL A WINDBREAK?

It is calculated that a windbreak is effective for up to six times its height. Therefore, if you have a 1.8 m (6 ft) barrier at one end of a 25 m (25 yd) long allotment, you will need another half way down to protect the whole plot.

On a smaller scale, you could make mini windbreaks with netting or hessian to protect individual rows of plants. Protection in the form of cloches and plastic coverings can also make a huge difference.

THE SOIL

Soil is the life force of gardening. It is made up of air, water, minerals and organic matter, the elements of rock formations eroded over the millennia. A thriving worm population is an excellent sign. Ideally, there should be a two or three worms on every spadeful you dig. Healthy soil has a wholesome, earthy smell.

Types of soil

The main categories of soils are sand, clay, silt and loam. There are also the chalk and peat types. Soils are classified according to the size of their particles.

+ **Sandy soil** has the biggest particles, visible to the naked eye. This makes it a free-draining 'light' soil, so nutrients are easily leached, or washed away. Sandy soil is easy to work and warms up quickly in spring. It is often low in potash.

+ **Clay soil** is made up of microscopic particles invisible to the naked eye. Sticky in texture, it is a slow-draining 'heavy' soil. The disadvantages are that it can become waterlogged, is sluggish to warm up in spring, tough going to dig and it cakes in the heat. The advantage is that minerals and nutrients don't get washed away easily.

+ **Silt** is an alluvial soil, typically from riverbanks, and lies somewhere between clay and sand. It is easily compacted but holds on quite well to nutrients.

+ **Loam** has the ideal balance of sand, silt and clay with the right amount of drainage as well as water and nutrient retention.

+ **Chalk** is a poor soil. It is free draining and low in nutrients. Chalk soil is full of lime, which makes it alkaline and inhospitable to many plants.

+ **Peat soil** occurs in wetlands and is light and easy to work, fertile but acid. It retains water when wet, but dries fast and has a tendency to blow away.

OBSERVING NATIVE PLANTS

You can tell a lot about the soil in the area by just looking around at the landscape and noting the native flora. An indication of rich and fertile soil is the presence of plenty of nettles, chickweed, goosegrass, thistles, groundsel and yarrow.

✦ **Acid soil** birch, broom, rowan, Scots pine, daisies, foxgloves, gorse, marestail, periwinkle, pansies, scabious.

✦ **Alkaline soil** hawthorn, hazel, cowslip, clematis, goat's beard, ox-eye daisies, valerian, wild carrot, yarrow.

✦ **Heavy clay** creeping buttercup, goosegrass, hoary plantain.

✦ **Light dry soil** nettles, brambles, broad leafed docks, dandelions, groundsel, chickweed, shepherd's purse.

✦ **Damp soil** alder, bugle, bulrush, buttercup, cuckoo flower, willow herb, plantain, primrose, ragged robin, thistle, willow.

Soil structure

In good soil, the particles clump together to form 'crumbs'. Air and water filtrate through the spaces between the crumbs to nourish the plants' roots. Worms can move easily through it, making channels while refining and improving the soil. The ideal soil has a 50:50 mix of crumbs and air spaces.

Soil profile

If you are being thorough, or have worries about drainage, it is worth digging a small hole around 90 cm (3 ft) deep. This will reveal horizontal bands – the topsoil, the subsoil, broken rock and the bedrock below.

Topsoil The first layer of topsoil is noticeably darker than the rest. It is this layer that feeds the plants. Most vegetables will be happy with 38 cm (15 in) of topsoil. Bush fruits need 45 cm (18 in) and most fruit trees need 60 cm (24 in). If you can see holes and cracks on the exposed face there is plenty of air going through. If not, then you need to open it up by adding organic matter or raising the beds.

Subsoil This is lighter in colour than topsoil. It contains few plant nutrients but its structure affects drainage. It is important that water can flow away and air can get to the plants' roots. Pour some water down the hole to see if it runs away. If it doesn't, it could be due to compacted airless topsoil or an impermeable barrier in the subsoil known as a hard 'pan'. This can usually be broken up with a pickaxe or loosened with a fork and kept aerated with regular additions of organic matter.

Acid or alkaline?

Some soils are too acid or too alkaline for plants to prosper, though this is rare except in extreme conditions. The micro-organisms needed to provide vital nutrients for the plants will not survive in either extreme. Acidity is measured on the pH (potential of Hydrogen) scale of 0–14. Neutral soil is the halfway house of pH7, below 7 is acid soil, and above 7 is alkaline. The optimum pH value for most plants is 5.5–7.5. Gardening centres sell cheap kits for checking soil.

DETERMINING YOUR SOIL TYPE

To work out your soil type, feel the texture. Sandy soil is gritty, silt feels silky and clay is sticky. Pick up a small handful 30 minutes after it has rained. If the soil will mould into a ball, it will be silt or clay. Clay goes shiny when rubbed. Sand will feel gritty and doesn't mould. Chalk will slip through your fingers while peat is dark and crumbly. For a more professional, in-depth analysis, send a sample off to be tested either with the Royal Horticultural Society or other specialist places advertised in gardening magazines.

Improving your soil

Every type of soil will be improved immeasurably by regularly incorporating organic matter in the form of well-rotted compost or manure. This will increase fertility, encourage worms and help with both drainage and water retention right across the board. The improved structure will help penetration of plant roots through the soil. While you may greatly improve your soil, you cannot completely change its character.

✦ **Chalk soil** Organic matter will help to bulk it up, add nutrients and counteract the alkaline pH.

✦ **Clay and silt soils** Piling in sharp sand, grit and organic matter will get air and some free-flowing drainage through it and make it workable. Raised beds will help because treading on clay or silt soil will compact it, making it airless. Dig it over in the autumn and allow winter weather to get at the soil to break it down.

✦ **Sandy soil** Adding well-rotted compost or manure will help to bind the particles together and retain nutrients and moisture. Leave any digging until spring and keep the soil covered through winter to minimize leaching.

✦ **Peat soil** Organic matter will give peat soil substance and weight.

✦ **Alkaline soil** If the soil is too alkaline, garden manure and compost will send it in the right direction.

THE VITAL ORGANIC ELEMENT IN SOIL

The vital nutrients in the soil needed for plant life are nitrogen (N), phosphorus (P), and potassium or potash (K), as well as the trace elements, particularly calcium, sulphur and magnesium. These are largely drawn from organic elements in the soil – decomposed vegetable and animal remains, fungi, algae, bacteria, and the millions of the micro-organisms that break it down. In its most developed form, it turns into humus, the greatest soil improver of all. Humus coats soil particles to make the crumbs. It holds onto water and prevents nutrients from leaching, or being washed away, by the rain.

✦ **Acid soil** If the soil is too acid, add lime. Ground limestone (calcium carbonate) and dolomitic limestone (calcium magnesium carbonate) are the organic choices. Do not add lime at the same time as manure as it will react against it. The general practice is to lime in autumn and manure in spring.

ORGANIC FERTILIZERS

+ **Blood, fish and bone** is a good general fertilizer. Quite quickly released. Spread it two weeks before the crops go in. Nitrogen 3.5%, phosphorus 8%, potassium 0.5%.

+ **Hoof and horn** is an excellent tonic for tired plants after winter. Apply at least two weeks before it is needed. Good source of slow release nitrogen. Nitrogen 13%.

+ **Dried blood** is the fastest acting nitrogen booster. Don't apply late in summer as it will encourage the plants to put out a lot of soft foliage that will be zapped by the frosts. Nitrogen 12–14%. A little phosphorus.

+ **Fish meal** is a good fertilizer for nitrogen and phosphorus combined. Nitrogen 9%, phosphorus 2.5%

+ **Bone meal** is very high in phosphorus so good for establishing roots particularly when planting trees or shrubs. Wear gloves when using. Nitrogen 3.5%, phosphorus 22%.

+ **Seaweed meal** has a wide range of trace elements and is a miracle all-round tonic. It is slow release and best used when the soil is warm. Rather expensive. Nitrogen 2.8%, phosphorus 0.2%, potassium 2.3%, plus trace elements.

+ **Rock potash** is the one for potassium. Potassium 10%.

+ **Wood ash** from your bonfire contains some potassium and potash depending on the wood. It has a very high pH so don't use it on alkaline soil. You could push it over the top.

+ **Dried animal manures** are good soil conditioners. They contain only small amounts of NPK but the full range of trace elements. Nitrogen 1%, phosphorus 1%, potassium 1.5%, plus trace elements.

+ **Liquid manures** are easily made on the allotment. You need a large barrel or drum filled with water, string, a hessian sack and a stout stick. Half fill the sack with manure, comfrey or nettles, tie it up at the neck and suspend it in the water from the stick for about two weeks. You can then use it straight onto the soil or dilute it by 50% if you want to spray it.

WEEDS

While weeds are a sign of soil fertility, it is essential to control them among food crops. They will compete with your plants for nutrients, light, space and water. On allotments, where watering is usually slow and painstaking, retaining moisture in the soil is of prime importance – particularly in the light of global warming and hot summers.

Some weeds are thugs, vigorous, greedy colonizers that will take over unless strictly controlled. Most annual and biennial weeds propagate themselves by seed, but the perennials are more resourceful. If grazing animals, frost, fire or man should destroy the top growth, they'll regenerate from the roots.

Controlling perennial weeds

With these weeds it is best to take firm action from the outset. The organic choices are to dig them out with every last bit of root, or to deprive them of light. On a new allotment digging them out is a daunting task. The best idea might be to cover the worst areas to deprive them of light and carefully and painstakingly dig over and filter through the borders that you want to plant first. Then you can gradually extend your territory. By the third year the weeds you have covered should be gone.

To cover an area of weeds, first scythe or strim down tall weeds. Cover the area with heavy black plastic buried at the edges and weighed down with stones or bricks. Though not all sites permit it as it contains chemicals and looks unsightly, hessian-backed carpet is widely used as an alternative. Avoid the foam-backed type as it will eventually break down and be difficult and unpleasant to remove.

Other possibilities for covering weeds are large sheets of heavy cardboard of the type used by removal, kitchen or bathroom appliance firms. You can also buy biodegradable cardboard and weed-suppressant material specially designed for the job.

The length of time you need to keep the cover on depends on the particular weed, but two to three years is the average. If you make holes to allow in water, you can plant through the cover by making cross slits. It is best to use plants that are a fair size and quite vigorous by nature, like potatoes or marrows.

Annual weed control

Annual weeds are much easier to control. They grow, flower, seed and die in the course of one year. They propagate themselves by producing quantities of seed, sometimes tens of thousands. To get on top of annual weeds it is vital to prevent them from flowering and setting seed. As the roots are generally in the top few centimetres of the soil, they can be kept down by hoeing and hand-pulling. Through the

good idea

Another way to beat the weeds is to give your plants a head start against the competition by transplanting or using pre-germinated or chitted seed.

THE STALE SEEDBED

One way to get ahead of annual weeds is to make a stale seedbed. Prepare the bed for planting and let the resulting weeds that have been brought to the surface germinate. If the weather is cold, warm the soil for a couple of weeks with polythene or fleece.

Hoe off the weeds before sowing your seed and with luck your seeds should be up before any more weeds have the chance to appear.

growing season, catch them young before they make too much root.

Seeds lurk dormant in the soil. When you dig and bring them up near the light they are likely to germinate – one reason for the 'no-dig system'. A 5 cm (2 in) depth of organic mulch on top of the soil between plants will dispose of most annual weeds by depriving them of light. A seed only has the resources to grow a little way to find the light it needs for photosynthesis. As the mulch is of loose texture, any rogue seedlings that make it through can be pulled out with

WEEDS FOR ZERO TOLERANCE

UNDERGROUND CREEPERS
These plants are vigorous and invasive.

+ **Bindweed** (*Convolvulus arvensis*)

+ **Ground elder** (*Aegopodium podagraria*)

+ **Couch grass** (*Agropyron repens*)

+ **Creeping thistle** (*Cirsium arvense*)

+ **Japanese knotweed** (*Polygonum cuspidatum*)

+ **Couch grass** (*Agropyron repens*, syn. *Elymus repens*)

SURFACE CREEPERS
These plants put down runners. When the stem touches the soil it makes roots.

+ **Brambles** (*Rubus*)

+ **Creeping buttercup** (*Rununculus repens*)

+ **Ground ivy** (*Glechoma hederacea*)

+ **Cinquefoil** (*Potentilla*)

WEEDS WITH TAP ROOTS
Tap roots are extremely difficult to dig out.

+ **Cow parsley** (*Anthriscus sylvestris*)

+ **Docks** (*Rumex*) If allowed to set seed, some docks can release 40,000 seeds.

UNDERGROUND RHIZOMES, TUBERS AND BULBS

+ **Horsetail** (*Equisetum arvense*)

+ **Oxalis** (*Oxalis*)

+ **Wild garlic** (*Allium vineale*)

ease. A good leaf cover of crops will also shade out annual weeds. Aim to keep the ground covered one way or another. While beds are empty cover them with mulch, polythene or other crop covers or sow a green manure crop to black them out.

The flame gun approach
Flame gunning has been used in agriculture since the 19th century. A flame gun is not designed to burn the weeds, but gives off the right heat for the cell structure to change and rupture the cell walls several hours later. You can tell if the treatment has been effective

FRIENDLY ANNUAL WEEDS

Some so-called weeds are useful as long as they are sited away from your crops in odd corners. They may put nitrogen into the soil or attract beneficial insects.

✦ **Black medick** (*Medicago lupulina*) Attractive to bees and butterflies. It enriches the soil through its nitrogen-fixing roots.

✦ **Chickweed** (*Stellaria media*) The seeds are good for birds.

✦ **Clover** (*Trifolium*) This is a nitrogen-fixing plant which enriches the soil.

✦ **Dandelion** (*Taraxacum officinale*) The leaves are good in salads. Coffee substitute can be made from the roots. It is attractive to butterflies and bullfinches.

✦ **Fat hen** (*Chenopodium album*) Attractive to hoverflies and bees, and can be eaten like spinach.

✦ **Nettles** (*Urtica dioica*) The young leaves can be cooked like spinach. Butterflies love it and it makes excellent fertilizer.

✦ **Red campion** (*Lychnis dioica*) Attractive to bees and butterflies. The night perfume draws in moths.

✦ **Toadflax** (*Linaria vulgaris*) Attractive to bees.

✦ **Teasel** (*Dipsacus fullonum*) Birds enjoy the seedheads.

by pressing a leaf between finger and thumb. If it has worked it will leave a dark green fingerprint.

Weeds are flame gunned at about 71°C (160°F) for a single second. In agriculture, flame gunning is generally used for clearing small weeds in the carefully calculated time between sowing a crop and the seeds emerging. It has the advantage of not disturbing the soil with the consequence of bringing more weed seed up to the light to germinate. Tough perennials may need several treatments. Obviously there are always dangers attached to fire and you may need permission to use a flame gun from your allotment site manager.

MAKING A PLAN

The beds

If you plan to grow vegetable crops, you will need four main beds in a rotation plan. The standard width is about 1.2 m (4 ft) to 1.35 m (4 ft 6 in) wide, depending on your reach. This will allow you to work on the beds from either side without treading on them and compacting the soil. Some people, however, prefer narrower beds about 90 cm (3 ft) wide as this is the most common width of fleece and crop covers, allowing for a border each side.

Vegetable beds are best run north to south so the vegetables don't shade each other. Put the taller vegetables and climbers at the north end. Any fruit trees could go behind them so as not to cast shade. The traditional length of a vegetable bed is about 9 m (30 ft), though this may be too long for the less serious grower.

Perennial vegetables and fruit can be slotted around the edges as most can take a little shade. Flower borders can be in sun or part shade depending on what you want to grow. Mediterranean herbs (basil, thyme, rosemary) will need full sun.

Paths

You will need paths all round the site, and a direct path to your shed. In practice, people inevitably take the shortest route even if it means trampling over precious crops or taking a flying leap over beds. A way round this is to put in some stepping stones or narrow gaps in the borders at tactical intervals.

You will need an arterial path to wheel weeds to the compost bins, to ferry manure about and to dive around the allotment

good idea

If you are planning to use a strip cropping programme, it's a good idea to take a tip from the market gardeners and to standardize the widths of borders. If all the beds are of a specific size or multiples of that size, the cloches and 'lights' will slot in over any bed in the allotment, giving you maximum flexibility.

PATHS

When starting out, leave a few options open as you may change your mind.

+ **Mown grass** makes a lovely path but it does need maintaining. Also it can become slippery and, for that reason, is not ideal in areas of heavy rainfall. If you are going for a grass path, make it the width or a multiple of the width, of the lawn mower.

+ **Trampled earth** is the simplest type of path. If weeds are a problem, obliterate them with black polythene, silage bags or a weed suppressant fabric. Black polypropylene sheeting will do the trick

---

yourself. A comfortable width for a main path is about 90 cm (3 ft) to allow for freedom of movement with a loaded barrow. Certainly it should be wide enough to set the barrow down and turn corners without tipping. It is worth trotting up and down with the barrow a few times to see what suits you.

Narrower paths are fine around the beds and along the periphery of the site to prune soft fruit, just allowing room to stand

comfortably. Some recommend as little 45 cm (18 in). However, keep in mind that plants often stick out beyond the edge of the beds.

The work area

More often than not, allotments come with a shed provided. This becomes the heart of your plot and your refuge from the elements. Tools, compost, fertilizers, fold-up chairs and other paraphernalia are kept in it, along with a primus stove to make tea.

Cold frames and nursery beds should be near the greenhouse or shed to make a convenient working area. Ideally, the nursery beds should be a useful size for your cloches or 'lights'. Extra backup is useful in the form of cold frames. Position these to be south facing.

The nursery or seedbed

The nursery or seedbed is useful for seedling crops and as a holding area for young plants before they go out into their permanent positions. Usually space is not a problem on the allotment, but the idea is to keep plants that don't mind being

good idea

Cold frames are truly invaluable for tender crops and for extending the season. Allow room on your plot for a good row of them in a sunny spot.

WATER

To encourage wildlife, consider putting in a little pond. It need be no bigger than a washing-up bowl. Even the smallest pond will draw in the birds to drink and wash. It is said that beneficial flies such as aphid midges double their egg production when there is a little water. If you can get some frogs to move in, they will effectively demolish the slug population.

transplanted away from the main beds until there is space for them and they need more room to grow. Leeks and most brassicas – particularly the slow-growing ones like Brussels sprouts – are traditional plants for this.

An easier alternative is to interplant (see page 87), thus avoiding transplanting and any danger of damaging the roots. A seedbed is useful as being the one small area that you can keep in tip-top condition fairly effortlessly. With glass over it or cloches, you can extend the season for a multitude of plants.

Siting organic matter

The manure heap This needs to be near the road for access. To get the heat up, make the heap as big as possible – 1.8 m (6 ft) square would be a good size. It's best to put this away from the shed where you will spend much of your time as it can be quite smelly until it rots down.

The compost bins Position at the bottom of the slope (if you have one) so the heavy loads go downhill. Three is ideal number: one brewing, one filling and one ready to go. They can smell rank until they rot down, so keep them away from where you sit.

Leafmould containers These are usually mesh bins. Leaves will take a year or so to rot down. Leafmould doesn't contain many nutrients but it is very good for improving soil texture.

FROM THEORY TO PRACTICE

Even the most highly trained and experienced garden designer needs to see how the plan on paper works out in practice, and may find they need to make a few changes on the ground. Your original paper plan is likely to be just a basis to work from, a starting off point.

Work it out roughly on paper, then mark out your plan on the ground. Ropes or washing lines are useful for getting a rough idea of how the division of the space, the general shapes and proportions are going to look and work in practice. Some people use spray paint to mark out the area. To get straight lines you will need a ball of string and some skewers. If you can, work off a straight edge like the corner of the shed. Tie the string through the eyelet of the skewer and plunge that into the ground. Use it as your point of reference and measure everything off from it.

Starting the makeover

Don't get discouraged if the tasks in hand appear to be monumental. Take it a step at a time. It's not a bad idea to put some of the plot out of action completely, especially if it is riddled with weeds, so you can concentrate on the most important areas first. Work out what you want to do with the plot and prioritise. Don't think in terms of unrealistic television makeovers. Plan to pull the plot round over a number of years. Make a wish list like the one shown opposite so you can work out what is going to be possible. The diagrams on the following pages show an example of a survey that you might draw up, followed by year-by-year 'action plans', showing how you can achieve this wish list.

Putting areas on hold

Taking the worst scenario of a really weedy and neglected site, make a three- to four-year plan. Put some areas temporarily out of action and work on others section by section.

Weedy areas and the work area
Cover these with a commercial weed-suppressant cover, black

plastic sheeting or silage bags. This is of three-fold benefit. It will give you time, effectively destroy bad weeds organically over a year or two, and you can plant through it. Weigh the plastic down with stones. You can cover it with wood shavings to make it look better. Most parks departments will supply wood shavings free to allotments sites. Get on to your site manager if he or she hasn't thought of it yet. You can plant vigorous growers like potatoes through slits in the polythene. A packet of marrow or squash seeds will cover a big area cheaply and look cheerfully ornamental.

Paths These can take much the same treatment. Very temporary paths can be made with heavy newspaper or cardboard covered with woodchip. When you are sure you have the paths where you want them, you may decide to think about a more permanent solution.

Other areas in waiting If you think you are not going to get round the whole allotment

straight away, plant a green manure crop. This will condition the soil and make good compost material for a minimum of effort on your part.

WISH LIST EXAMPLE

+ Four big beds for a good quantity of traditional fresh vegetables

+ Asparagus bed

+ Raspberries for summer and autumn

+ Blackberries

+ Gooseberries

+ Strawberries

+ Espaliered pears

+ Herbs

+ Flowers

+ A wildflower area

+ A place to sit in the evening sun

The Survey

The soil is slightly acidic clay, pH 6.5. There is quite a good worm population. Drainage is fair, but the soil could do with opening up with some organic material. There is a soggy corner on the west side of the shed. Consider raised beds here. The prevailing winds are not strong but are from the south-west. There is a very bad patch of bindweed and ground elder along most of the east border.

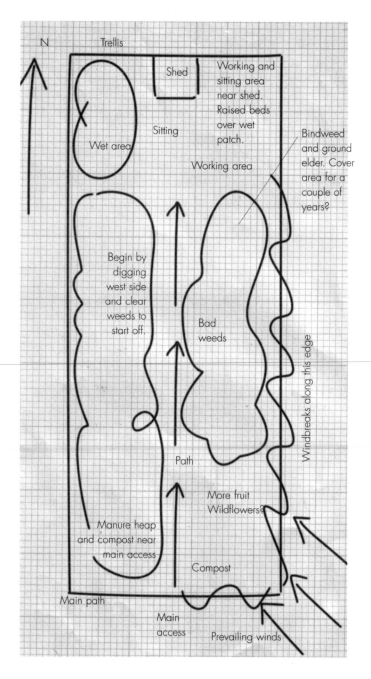

Year One

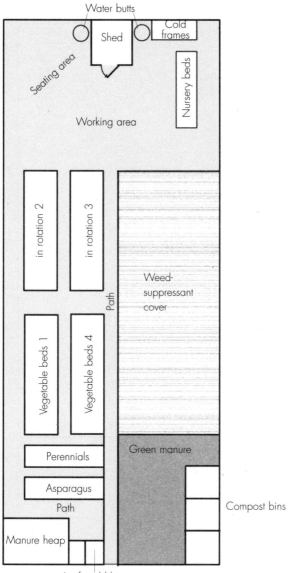

Three-quarters of the plot is covered either with weed-suppressant material or with green manure.

JOBS

Put the weedy side under black plastic covered with wood shavings. Grow potatoes through it. Borrow petrol strimmer to strim down the weeds. Get hold of silage bags from friend in the country. Talk to the site manager to see if he can get wood chips from the Parks Department. Cover the working area and make paths.
Construct compost bins. Start manure, leafmould and compost heaps.
Find a source of horse manure.
Mark out, weed and clear beds for vegetables on the other side.
Sow green manure.

Year Two

Half the plot is covered
with weed-suppressant
material.

JOBS
Keep the weed-infested
area under cover, but sow
marrows and squashes
through it.
Visit fruit nursery and get
advice on espaliers and
raspberries.
Put up supports ready for
the fruit, then plant them.
Dig up green manure and
plant gooseberry bushes.
Through winter, build
raised beds with trellis
behind in the sitting area.
This will be a suntrap for
the evenings to relax and
read the papers. Plants will
be aromatic herbs and
scented flowers at nose
height – lavender and
lilies?

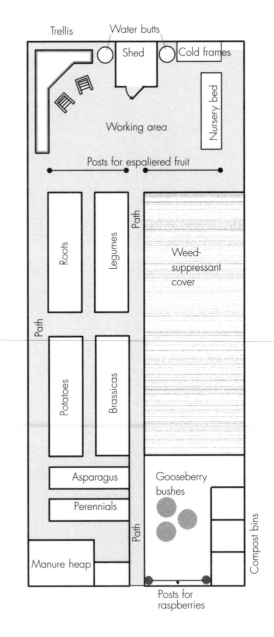

Year Three or Four

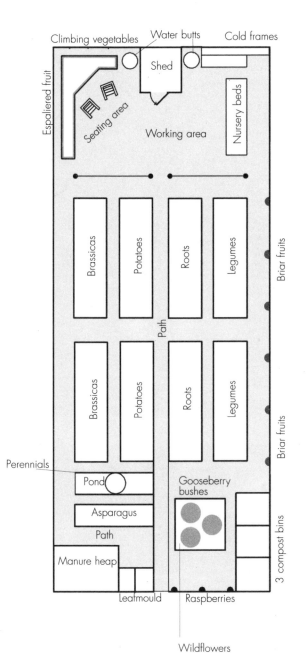

Only paths, and the sitting and working areas are covered with weed-suppressant material.

JOBS
Lift the weed-suppressant cover off what was the weedy area and make more beds for vegetables. Put up posts and wires for blackberries and hybrids along the east side. Make a small pond and sow some wildflowers to encourage wildlife and beneficial insects.

CHAPTER

3

the
plants

Once the stage is set, you are ready to choose your cast of vegetables, fruits and flowers. Which are most suited to your plot and how will you organize them? The rotation system is explained with lists of the plants most suited to different types of soil. Fruit can be trained to give blossom and structure as well as produce. Flowers and herbs are good for biodiversity.

CHOOSING WHAT TO GROW

Although the law lays down that allotments should be used mostly for growing produce, these days most allotment committees or managers take a fairly liberal view – just so long as people look after their plots and are not a nuisance to anyone else. It is lovely to see the variety of interests in the plots. You may find allotment holders specializing in growing plants for dying cloth, flowers for botanical painting, unusual salads and herbs, or even a little vineyard for wine.

Depending on the bye-laws, some allotments allow hens, rabbits and beekeeping. In the North of England, you will find a grand tradition of pigeon fanciers and pot leeks competitions. Prize-winning dahlias, chrysanthemums and sweet peas are also allotment classics. However, for the vast majority of people, top of the list are still fresh vegetables and fruit.

Be realistic when you plan what to grow. Work out what is practical for you and your way of life. Take into consideration the condition of your plot, the time available and the appetite of your family. The commonest mistake is to grow so much of the same things that you end up with a glut and they end up on the compost heap – truly a waste of effort.

Decide if you want to grow all the produce that you and your family can eat. Perhaps you would prefer to concentrate on those vegetables that are difficult to find, expensive to buy, taste so much better home-grown, or are your particular passion?

VEGETABLES

When thinking about growing vegetables, you need to work out a rotation for the annuals. These are the vast majority, the ones that you will sow and harvest within one year, often within one season. As families of plants share the same weaknesses and are prone to the same problems, the principle is to group them together and move them to fresh soil every year to help prevent a build-up of soil-borne pests and disease.

There are four commonly grown major groups, or families, of vegetables – potatoes, roots (the carrot family), legumes (the pea and bean family) and brassicas (the cabbage family). The normal practice is to make four permanent beds and move each family group to the next bed every year. The groups always move in the same order and direction, ending up where they started in the fourth year.

Two of the groups benefit from the soil being limed and the other two from manuring. As lime makes the soil alkaline and manure makes it acid, the alternate treatments keep the soil balanced and in good heart. Changing the crops from deep rooting to shallow is also good for soil structure. The whole idea works like clockwork. As you only have to treat each small area as needed, following the rotation scheme will save you money, time and effort.

How rotation works

Year one: Potatoes Potatoes are known as a 'clearing crop' as they take quite a bit of excavating. All the digging exposes pests to the birds. They also put out plenty of leaf cover to smother weeds. The plot is dug over and well manured before they are planted as they like rich soil slightly on the acid side.

Year two: Roots The soil left by the potatoes with year-old manure is about right for roots as they will fork in too rich a soil. A light dressing of lime before planting will raise the pH as roots like soil on the alkaline side.

THE ROTATION PROGRAMME

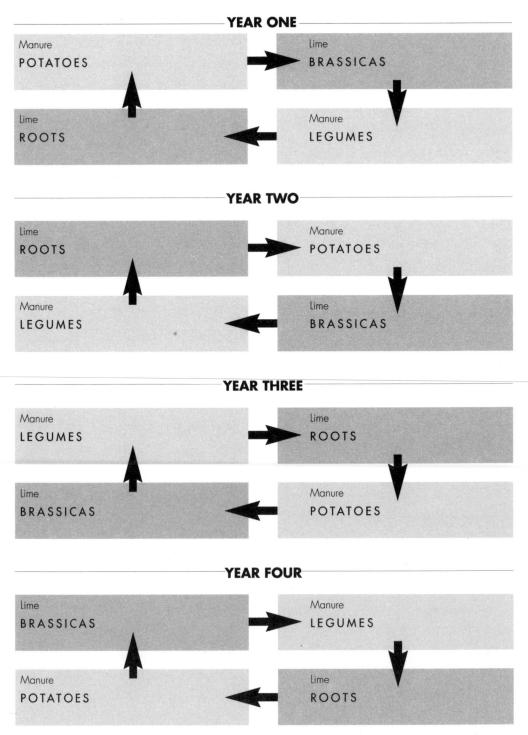

YEAR ONE

Manure
POTATOES

Lime
BRASSICAS

Lime
ROOTS

Manure
LEGUMES

YEAR TWO

Lime
ROOTS

Manure
POTATOES

Manure
LEGUMES

Lime
BRASSICAS

YEAR THREE

Manure
LEGUMES

Lime
ROOTS

Lime
BRASSICAS

Manure
POTATOES

YEAR FOUR

Lime
BRASSICAS

Manure
LEGUMES

Manure
POTATOES

Lime
ROOTS

Year three: Legumes Add another dressing of manure before planting the legumes. The pea and bean tribe have nitrogen-fixing roots so they enrich into the soil. As nitrogen is good for leaf growth, it is logical that the leafy brassicas, planted in year four, will benefit as the last in the succession.

Year four: Brassicas A top-dressing of lime will give them some protection against clubroot as it thrives in acid soil.

If you are unfortunate enough to get a bad blight – eelworm or clubroot left in the soil – it is best to avoid planting the vulnerable family for as many years as possible. The extended family charts are useful in that if a crop fails to prosper due to soil-borne diseases or pests, you will know to avoid planting any other family members there – tomatoes or aubergines in the potato patch for example, or swedes in the brassica bed.

Once you have your four beds, other families may share with them. Often onions are grown with legumes, for example. The salads and most of the other vegetables are fitted in where there is room. Keep maturing times in mind as you will want to clear the ground and prepare it for the next crop.

Perennial vegetables

The perennials – artichokes and cardoons, scorzonera and perpetual spinach among them – need separate beds where they won't be disturbed by the annual quadrille. They can go in with flowers and the tall ones can be intercropped (see page 87). Asparagus needs its own carefully prepared bed with good drainage and a generous depth of topsoil where it can settle and keep cropping for twenty years.

Soil preferences

The majority of vegetables prefer free-draining soils on the light, sandy side rather than the heavier clays. Legumes, roots, fruits (tomatoes, peppers, aubergine, sweetcorn and so on), cucurbits (cucumbers, courgettes, squash, pumpkins and marrows), onions, the beetroot family (which includes spinach of all types)

FAMILY CHARTS

LEGUMES (PAPILLIONACEAE)
Asparagus pea (*Lotus tetragonolobus*)
Broad bean (*Vicia faba*)
French bean (*Phaseolus vulgaris*)
Lab lab bean (*Lablab purpureus*)
Lima or butter bean (*Phaseolus lunatus*)
Mangetout (*Pisum sativum*)
Peas (*Pisum sativum*)
Runner bean (*Phaseolus coccineus*)
Sugar snap peas (*Pisum sativum*)
Yard long beans (*Vigna unguiculata* subsp. *sesquipedelis*)

BRASSICAS (BRASSICACEAE)
American land cress (*Barbarea verna*)
Broccoli, sprouting (*Brassica oleraceae* Italica Group)
Broccoli, perennial (*Brassica oleracea* Italica Group)
Broccoli, Chinese (*Brassica oleracea* var. *algoglabra*)
Brussels sprouts (*Brassica oleracea* Gemmifera Group)
Cabbage (*Brassica oleracea* Capitata Group)
Calabrese (*Brassica oleracea* Italica Group)
Cauliflower (*Brassica oleracea* Botrytis Group)
Chinese cabbage (*Brassica rapa* var. *pekinensis*)
Chrysanthemum greens (*Brassica campestris chinensis* var. *utilis*)
Kale (*Brassica oleracea* Acephela Group)
Kohlrabi (*Brassica oleracea* Gongylodes Group)
Komatsuna (*Brassica rapa* var. *perviridis* or var. *komatsuna*)
Mizuna greens (*Brassica rapa* var. *nipposinica*)
Mustard greens (*Brassica juncea*)
Pak choi (*Brassica rapa* var. *chinensis*)
Radish (*Raphanus sativus* Longipinnatus Group)
Rocket (*Eruca versicaria*)
Seakale (*Crambe maritima*)
Swede (*Brassica napus* Napobrassica Group)
Texcel greens (*Brassica carinata*)
Turnip (*Brassica rapa* Rapifera Group)

POTATO FAMILY (SOLANACEAE)
Aubergine (*Solanum melongena*)
Peppers, sweet (*Capsicum annuum* Grossum Group)
Peppers, chilli (*Capsicum annuum* Longum Group)
Potato (*Solanum tuberosum*)
Tomato (*Lycopersicon esculentum*)

ROOTS (APIACEAE)
Carrot (*Daucus carota*)
Celeriac (*Apium graveolens* var. *rapaceum*)
Celery (*Apium graveolens* var. *rapaceum*)
Chervil, turnip-rooted (*Chaerophyllum bulbosum*)
Florence fennel (*Foeniculum vulgare*)

FAMILY CHARTS

Hamburg parsley (*Petroselinum crispum*
var. *tuberosum*)
Parsley (*Petroselinum*)
Parsnip (*Pastinaca sativa*)

CHENOPODIACEAE
Beetroot (*Beta vulgaris* subsp. *vulgaris*)
Chard (*Beta vulgaris* Cicla Group)
Good King Henry (*Chenopodium bonus-
henricus*)
Perpetual spinach (*Beta vulgaris* subsp.
Chenopodiaceae)
Red orache (*Atriplex hortensis*)
Spinach (*Spinacia oleracea*)
Spinach beet (*Beta vulgaris* Cicla Group)

ALLIACEAE
Garlic (*Allium sativum*)
Globe onion (*Allium cepa*)
Japanese bunching onion (*Allium
fistulosum*)
Leek (*Allium porrum*)
Pickling onion (*Allium cepa*)
Shallots (*Allium cepa* Aggregatum
Group)
Spring onion (*Allium cepa*)
Tree onion (*Allium cepa* Prolifera Group)
Welsh onion (*Allium fistulosum*)

CUCURBITACEAE
Courgettes (*Cucurbita pepo*)
Cucumber (*Cucumis sativus*)
Gherkins (*Cucumis sativus*)
Marrows (*Cucurbita pepo*)
Melon (*Cucumis melo*)

Pumpkin (*Cucurbita maxima*)
Squash, summer (*Cucurbita pepo*)
Squash, winter (*Cucurbita moschata*)

ASTERACEAE
Cardoon (*Cynara cardunculus*)
Celtuce (*Lactuca sativa* var. *augustana*)
Chicory (*Chicorium intybus*)
Endive (*Cichorium endivia*)
Globe artichoke (*Cynara scolymus*)
Jerusalem artichoke (*Helianthus tuberosus*)
Lettuce (*Lactuca sativa*)
Salsify (*Tragopogon porrifolius*)
Scorzonera (*Scorzonera hispanica*)

ODD ONES OUT
Amaranth (*Amaranthus* sp.
Amaranthiaceae)
Asparagus (*Asparagus officinalis*,
Asparagaceae)
Borage (*Boraginaceae*)
Burdock (*Arctium lappa, Compositae*)
Chinese artichoke (*Stachys affinis*,
Lamiaceae)
Corn salad (*Valerianella locusta*,
Valerianaceae)
Okra (*Hibiscus esculentus, Malvaceae*)
Purslane (summer) (*Portulaca oleracea*,
Portulacaceae)
Rhubarb (*Rheum* x *cultorum*,
Polygonaceae)
Sorrel (*Rumex acetosa, Polygonaceae*)
Sweetcorn (*Zea mays, Poaceae*)
Sweet potato (*Convulaceae*)

prefer lighter soils. Brassicas are the one group that like firm clay soil for stability and to prevent wind rock. It's important that the light soils hold sufficient moisture and the heavy ones are free draining.

Looking at pH preferences (see opposite), or the acid/alkaline scale, generally you can't go wrong with neutral soil of pH7. However, the cucurbits do best in a slightly acid soil of pH5.5–7. The ideal range for potatoes is even more acid at pH 5–6. Cranberries like soil so acid that it's only possible to grow them in the UK in containers with special compost. The onion family, on the other hand, needs a neutral

good idea

For a little privacy, you can make a great summer screen by planting Jerusalem artichokes. They'll shoot up leaf cover to 2m (6ft) or more in a single season. A block of sweetcorn will do much the same in late summer or early autumn. A seating place under a screen of sunflowers is quite romantic and Provençal.

to alkaline soil on the high side of pH7 as do the brassicas.

You can tip the balance either way with top-dressings like lime and manure. If you need a different type of soil altogether to suit the crops you want to grow, raise the beds (see page 133) and fill them with the right kind of compost.

HERBS

Most of the common culinary herbs are easy to grow, indispensable in the kitchen and expensive to buy so it is well worth allowing some space for them. The aromatic Mediterranean types like rosemary are lovely to brush against, while thyme can take a little treading. Position near where you sit so you can benefit from the scent.

PLANTS FOR LIGHT, SANDY, FREE-DRAINING SOIL

Amaranthus (for best results)
Artichoke, globe
Aubergine
Beetroot
Burdock
Cardoon
Carrots
Celery
Celtuce
Chicory
Chilli
Corn salad (though not fussy)
Courgette (best at pH 5.5–7)
Cucumber, outdoor (prefers acidity of
    pH 5.5–7)
Endive
Florence fennel
French bean
Garlic
Hamburg parsley
Lablab or hyacinth bean
Leeks

Lettuce
Marrow (best at pH 5.5–7)
Okra
Onions – all, but particularly from seed
    (best at over pH7)
Orache (though not fussy)
New Zealand spinach
Parsnips
Peppers
Pumpkin (best at pH 5.5–7)
Radiccio
Radish
Runner beans
Salsify
Scorzonera
Seakale
Squash (best at pH 5.5–7)
Spinach
Spinach beet
Sweetcorn
Sweet potato
Yard long bean

PLANTS FOR HEAVY, CLAY SOIL

Brassicas (like firm soil with good
    drainage; dislike acid soils)
Broccoli
Brussels sprouts
Cabbage
Cauliflower
Chinese broccoli
Chinese cabbage
Kale

Kohlrabi
Komatsuna or mustard spinach
Mizuna and mibuna greens (they are not
    too fussy)
Mustard greens
Swede
Texcel greens
Turnips

FRUIT

Fruit is great value in terms of the triple performance of blossom, structure and fruit. Generally, fruit is trouble free once it's established and it lasts for many years. Few allotments allow trees to be grown as they shade other plots and sometimes cannot be moved for a new tenancy. Many, however, will allow trained fruit trees on dwarf rootstocks. Look for trees that have been certified by Defra (Department of the Environment, Food and Rural Affairs) Certification Scheme. Not all, but most of the commonly grown top fruits – apples, pears and plums – can carry the certificates to say that they are healthy, vigorous and true to variety. The same scheme applies

to all the soft fruits with the exception of red- and whitecurrants.

In the UK, tender fruits such as peaches, figs and apricots may need protection. Strawberries are treated differently from the other fruits as they are a short-term crop and are generally moved every three years to a new site. As they don't take up much room, strawberries can be slotted in almost anywhere.

Positioning fruit

Fruit trees and bushes are fairly permanent and need to be planned as part of the structure of the allotment. Avoid a windy site as most fruit trees are pollinated by insects. Although most fruit is tolerant of a wide range of soils, the ideal is a slightly acid loam (about pH6.5). Good drainage and a fair depth of topsoil are also important: most fruit trees need about 60 cm (24 in) of topsoil, while cherries need more (up to 75 cm/30 in), and bush fruits less (about 45 cm/18 in).

note

Apples, pears and plums lend themselves to being trained flat as pyramids, stopovers, espaliers, cordons or fans. For best results, site them in a sheltered sunny spot.

THE HEIGHT OF FRUIT TREES

Most fruit trees are grafted onto specific rootstocks to control the size and to make them come true to the variety. For example, with apples there is:

+ M27 An extremely dwarfing root-stock. These trees bear fruit within two or three years of planting but need support throughout their life and general cosseting.
+ M9 A very dwarfing rootstock. A less extreme version of the M27.
+ M26 A dwarfing rootstock. This creates a stronger small tree, good for low cordons and dwarf pyramids.
+ MM106 A semi-dwarfing rootstock. This is the standard size for trained trees.
+ MM111 and M2 rootstocks make big trees.

This is a complicated subject. Take advice from the tree nursery as to which rootstock you need for the ultimate size you want. Each type of fruit tree has different rootstock codes.

good idea

When buying fruit trees, ask the nursery about pollinators. Some trees, like the Victoria plum, are self-pollinating though they do better with a pollinator. Most need a different variety of the same type of fruit tree nearby – one that will blossom at the same time. Often the varieties on the wild side make the best pollinators – crab apples as partners for apples and the bitter morello cherry for cherry trees.

Most tree fruits can take some deal of shade but sunshine is needed to ripen the wood and the fruit, especially the sweet dessert fruits. Soft fruits need sunshine for half the day. Redcurrants, gooseberries, raspberries, blackcurrants, blackberries and hybrids, as well as summer raspberries, do well in part shade but do even better in sun. Autumn raspberries must have full sun. When choosing cultivars, keep in mind the likelihood of frost damage in spring. If you are in a cold area, choose late-flowering and frost-resistant varieties.

Soft fruit

Soft fruit is on the whole easier to care for than trained fruit trees. Be sure to get certified virus-free stock. Don't plant where the same fruit has been grown in the last seven years as they can get reversion disease. If you plan to grow a lot of fruit, consider putting up a fruit frame (if allowed by the allotment committee) to protect the fruit from birds.

Blackcurrants are grown as bushes and need plenty of space, growing up 1.8 m (6 ft) high and wide.

Redcurrants, whitecurrants and gooseberries are generally grown as bushes but they can be turned into a cordon, or even an espalier or fan, or they can be trained over an arch.

Blackberries and their hybrids need training against a structure, otherwise they will get into a tangle of thorns. If using a post and wire system, plan for the posts to be 3.6–4.5 m (12–15 ft) apart.

Raspberries Summer and autumn raspberries also need to be grown against a framework, usually a

BIRDS

It is the allotment holders's privilege to be able to encourage the birds. They should be fed all year round. They repay us by keeping us company and demolishing pests – particularly the voracious soil-borne pests lurking beneath the surface. However, when they become a bit too keen on our fruit, the best defence is netting. The cheap plastic type is the most hardwearing. It can just be draped over bushes or supported with stakes topped with jam jars to prevent the net ripping.

post and wire system with posts at 3–3.6 m (10–12 ft) apart.

Strawberries fit in any sunny border and are moved around on a three-year cycle.

Blueberries need such acid soil (pH 4–5.5) that they are best grown in special compost in containers.

FLOWERS

I hope that you will grow some flowers in your allotment, both to enjoy there, and to cut and take home. It is also worth growing flowers purely for practical purposes. Some flowers attract the insects that will demolish the pest population. The best-known beneficial insects are ladybirds and lacewings. Their larvae devour aphids and other soft-bodied pests in vast quantities.

There are also numerous other lesser-known flying insects that are equally good at keeping the bugs at bay. Parasitic wasps are small, sometimes so tiny you would hardly notice them. They lay their eggs on the larvae of other insects (aphids and cutworms among others) to provide a food for their young when they hatch out.

Unlike the unsavoury housefly, which spreads decayed and germ-ridden matter wherever it lands, adult parasitic flies live on the purest diet of nectar, pollen and the honeydew left by aphids. It is the newly hatched young that are carnivorous and devour caterpillar pests sometimes from the inside out. The syrphid fly, otherwise known as the hover fly or flower fly, camouflages itself as a wasp but is quite harmless to all except to pest larvae.

These helpful insects can be encouraged to settle in if given the kind of flowers that they most enjoy. Guaranteed to delight these tiny insects are the small flowers in proportion to themselves. Those of the carrot family are top favourites. Apart from the carrot itself, these include its wild forbear Queen Anne's Lace (*Daucus carota*), coriander (*Coriandrum*), fennel (*Foeniculum*), dill (*Anethum*), parsnip (*Pastinaca sativa*) and parsley (*Petroselinum*). Apart from coriander these are all biennial, so you won't get flowers until the second year. If you are growing the herbs anyway, you can just leave a few to flower the following year and then you will also have the opportunity of collecting the seed if you wish to do so.

The mint family (*Labiatae* and *Lamiaceae*) is also popular with

ATTRACTING INSECTS WITH A POND

A small source of water is said to double the egg production of some beneficial insects, especially in dry summers. If you don't have a pond or pool nearby, set a shallow dish into the ground. The ideal spot would catch the morning sun. Fill it almost to the top with pebbles or gravel and top with 0.5 cm (1/4 in) of water. Some pebbles poking out will enable the insects to scramble out should they suffer the misfortune of getting pulled under by the surface tension of the water.

good idea

Some of the wild flowers bees most enjoy can only be got from specialist wildflower seed nurseries. If you are not planning a wild flower meadow, look for the simple varieties of flowers that you want to grow anyway. Pick out varieties that are not too far removed through breeding from the wild forms.

beneficial insects and includes all the mints and thymes, as well as beebalm (*Monarda didyma*). These plants are easy to grow and don't take up much space, though mint needs to be curtailed from its colonizing habit by being contained in a bottomless bucket. The parasitic wasps and flies also love the tiny, hairy, white flowers of horehound (*Marrubium vulgare*).

As with bees, the predatory flies and wasps are greatly drawn to the daisy family (*Compositae* and *Asteraceae*). Though the flowers may seem large, they are actually composed of many small flowers in a ray and disc formation. Among this group is yarrow (*Achillea millefolium*), *Cosmos*, sunflowers and the old allotment favourite, dahlias.

Bees for pollination

Bees are invaluable in the allotment for pollinating crops. Bumblebees choose flowers to fit the length of their tongues. The bee with the longest tongue, *Bombus hortorum*, will reach into the heart of the deep tubular flowers of honeysuckle and foxgloves. While most wouldn't attempt it, *Bombus terrestris* gets round the disadvantage of a short tongue by biting through the side of flowers.

Many of the vegetables you grow anyway will attract bees if you leave the odd one to flower. They like the flowers of all the brassicas, broad beans and runner beans, asparagus, also herbs including borage, sage, lavender, rosemary, marjoram, all the mints and thymes. They enjoy the flowers of cucumbers and all members of the marrow (Cucurbit) family.

The parsnip flower is a top favourite with bees. They also seek out artichokes and cardoons, as well as the blossom of gooseberries and apple and pear trees. They love the bramble family, blackberries and their hybrids. Many plants that you grow for practical reasons also attract bees, including many of the green manure plants, particularly red clover (*Trifolium pratense*). They adore comfrey (*Symphytum*), worth growing for making great liquid manure.

Think of old-fashioned cottage garden flowers, pollen-rich varieties with single rather than double blooms. Low-growing plants are best sown in sunny sheltered spots in patches rather than dot planted. Bees are reputed to be particularly attracted to blue and white flowers.

Edible flowers

One of the great joys of growing your own is that you have a supply of delicacies that you wouldn't find in the shops, usually because they don't store well. Into this category must fall edible flowers. They always look wonderfully chic and extravagant in salads. There is a certain neatness about making every plant on the allotment useful and part of an edible landscape.

✦ The vivid blue flowers of borage taste of cucumber. They make a striking garnish to salads and summer drinks.

✦ The pot marigold, Calendula, can be used in the same way as saffron to colour cooked dishes or sprinkled on salads to brighten them up.

✦ Nasturtium flowers have a peppery taste and their bright orange flowers look good in salads.

BEE PLANTS

JAN	FEB	MAR	APR	MAY	JUN	JUL	AUG	SEP	OCT	NOV	DEC

Hellebores (*helleborus*)

Christmas box (*Sarcococca*)

Glory-in-the snow (*Chionodoxa luciliae*)

Crocus

Snowdrops (*Galanthus*)

Winter aconite (*Eranthis hyemalis*)

Daffodil (*Narcissus*)

Scilla siberica

Grape hyacinth (*Muscari*)

Strawberry (*Fragonia*)

Columbine (*aquilegia*)

Wallflower (*Erysimum*)

Dill (*Anethum graveolens*

Jacob's ladder (*Polemonium caeruleum*)

Honesty (*Lunaria annua*)

Bugle (*Ajuga*)

Thyme (*Thymus vulgaris*)

Foxglove (*Digitalis purpurea*)

Mallow (*Malva*)

Veronica longifolia

Poached egg plant (*Limnanthes douglasii*)

Love-in-a-mist (*Nigella damascena*)

Cornflower (*Centaurea cyanus*)

Lemon balm (*Melissa officinalis*)

Salvia (*Salvia splendens*)

Borage (*Boragp officinalis*)

Verbena bonariensis

Salvia superba

Bellflower (*Campanula latifolia*)

Lovage (*Levisticum officinalis*)

Peppermint (*Mentha piperita*)

Marjoram (*Origanum vulgaris*)

Goldenrod (*Solidago*)

Bee balm (*Monarda didyma*)

Winter savory (*Satureja montana*)

Cosmos

Hyssop (*Hyssopus officinalis*)

Sunflower (*Helianthus annuus*)

Hollyhock (*Alcea rosea*)

Dahlia

Globe thistle (*Echinops ritro*)

Aster

Coneflower (*Rudbeckia*)

Japanese anemone (*Anemone x hybrida*)

Hellebores (*Helleborus*)

✦ Chrysanthemum greens, *Brassica campestris chinensis* var. *utilis* (the 'edible chrysanthemum'), is a popular green vegetable in Japan and the flowers are used for sprinkling on stews, soups and salads.

✦ Young dandelion flowers are good for bitter salads if picked when young. Varieties have been cultivated to be less bitter.

✦ Courgette flowers are delicious fried in batter, tempura style. All the marrow family produce edible flowers. Daylilies can be treated in the same way.

✦ The flowers of herbs like hyssop, basil, bee balm, dill, fennel and garlic can be added to any dish that you are flavouring with the leaves.

✦ The violet flowerheads of chives are pretty in salads.

✦ Ornamental flowering plants with good leaves can be used for herbal tea.

✦ Candied pansies, violets and rosebuds look delightfully Edwardian on cakes and puddings.

✦ The pretty South African pelargoniums (not to be confused with geraniums) have leaves that taste variously of peppermint (*Pelargonium tomentosum*), lemon (*P. citronellum & P. crispum*) and roses (*P. graveloens*).

A word of warning: do not eat any flower unless you are positive that you know what it is and that it is safe to eat. Avoid any flowers that have been treated with pesticides or come from florists, nurseries or roadsides. As a general rule, only eat the petals.

GREEN MANURES

Green manures are very useful to the allotment holder, especially when taking over a new plot that is going to take a couple of years to sort out. They are fast-growing crops which are put in the ground for between six weeks to a year, depending on the type.

The short-term types are fast-growing leafy plants that can be slotted in six to eight week gaps when the ground is cleared between crops. These include fenugreek, mustard, phacelia and buckwheat. The over-wintering green manures – winter tare, grazing rye, winter beans and Italian ryegrass – are sown in early autumn when many vegetables are lifted. They will be dug into the soil the following spring. Long-term green manures – alfalfa, red clover and trefoil – can be left in the ground for a whole year, but should be clipped occasionally to stop them going woody.

Green manures are cut down before they flower or when you need the ground. Dig them up, chopping up the foliage with a spade as you go to speed up decomposition. Leave them to wilt for a few days on the surface of the soil before burying them by single digging. If you are on the no-dig system, leave the residue on the surface to act as a mulch, or compost it. Some of the perennials (clover, trefoil and rye) may grow again and will need to be hoed off or covered with mulch.

Types of green manure

Alfalfa (*Medicago sativa*) is a fast-growing leafy crop, a hardy perennial that fixes nitrogen. It grows tall, to 80 cm (32 in), and prefers alkaline soil. Being deep rooting, it can bring up nutrients from the depths and will help to

good idea

When choosing a green manure, keep in mind rotation (see page 47). The winter beans and lupins are legumes, while mustard and fodder radish are brassicas.

break up heavy soil. For the same reason it can cope with dry conditions once established. It is planted for a full season, either spring to autumn or late summer to spring. The young leaves can be eaten.

Buckwheat (*Fagopyrum esculentum*) is a half-hardy annual, 90 cm (3 ft) tall. Sow in April to harvest by autumn. It has deep roots and is good for weed smothering. Easy to dig in and copes with poor soil. The flowers are pretty and draw in helpful predators.

Crimson clover (*Trifolium incarnatum*) is a hardy annual. It has nitrogen-fixing roots. Though not too fussy, it does better on light soil. It is sown in spring and cut down by autumn, or it can be sown in late summer and overwintered. Flowers are relished by bees.

Red clover (*Trifolium pratense*) is a hardy perennial, growing to 30 cm (12 in). Clover is a nitrogen fixer and is loved by bees, so leave a few to flower. Sow in spring to late summer and grow for two or

BENEFITS OF GREEN MANURES

✦ They will usefully occupy the land until you are ready to cultivate it, making temporary cover and helping to keep the area free of weeds.

✦ They will prevent light soils from eroding and being leached by rain.

✦ Some green manures (for example, buckwheat and Italian ryegrass) have root systems that will help to break up heavy ground.

✦ The leguminous ones (clovers, winter beans and trefoil, and lupins) store nitrogen in their roots, which is released into the soil as they rot down.

✦ If you leave a few plants of phacelia, buckwheat and lupins to flower they will attract beneficial insects.

✦ Long-term green manures – alfalfa, red clover and trefoil – are useful for resting overused soil, improving fertility or giving you a break.

three months, or leave in the soil over the winter. It fixes nitrogen and is fairly easy to dig in. Red clover prefers light soils. Don't use clovers repeatedly as the land may become 'clover sick'.

Fenugreek (*Trigonella foenum-graecum*) is a half-hardy annual, growing to 60 cm (24 in) in height. These are bushy plants with weed-suppressing foliage, and possibly the best fast grower and nitrogen fixer for summer. Plant in late spring or summer in well-drained, fertile soil and grow for up to three months.

Lupin (*Lupinus angustifolius*), the agricultural variety of lupin, is a half-hardy annual, sown in spring for a slow-maturing summer crop. It takes two to three months to get to the digging stage and does best in light acid soil. Seeds are sown rather than broadcast, about 13 cm (5 in) apart. Deep rooting, they improve soil texture, are nitrogen fixing and effective in suppressing weeds. If left to flower, they are very attractive to beneficial predators. A big disadvantage is that they are poisonous.

Mustard (*Sinapsis alba*) is a tender, extremely fast-growing annual for

summer. You can dig it in after three weeks. It likes moist fertile soil.

Phacelia (*Phacelia tanacetifolia*) is a semi-hardy annual growing up to 90 cm (3 ft) tall with ferny leaves. Its bright blue flowers are attractive to beneficial insects, so leave a few for them. Plant after dangers of frost and grow for a couple of months. Last sowings in August. It will thrive in most soils and is easy to dig in.

Ryegrasses Grazing rye (*Secale cereale*) and Italian ryegrass (*Lollium multiflorum*) are hardy annuals used for overwintering and can take almost any soil. They need a couple of months to rot down and are likely to re-sprout. Not the easiest to dig in as they have tough fibrous roots. The best time to dig them in is when you can feel the flower heads swelling inside the stems. They are said to suppress wireworm.

Trefoil (*Medicago lupilina*) is a hardy biennial, growing to 30 cm (12 in) tall. It is a summer grower or, if sown in August, it can overwinter. It is nitrogen fixing, and one of the few that can cope with some shade and drought. It dislikes heavy acid soils.

Winter field bean (*Vicia faba*) is a hardy annual, growing to 90 cm (3 ft) tall. This broad bean is grown by farmers for animal feed. It fixes nitrogen, makes plenty of organic matter and is very hardy. Plant between September and November to overwinter in moist loam. It is moderately easy to dig in. Don't forget to leave the

nitrogen-rich roots. An excellent green manure that you can harvest and eat. Dry-seed for the following year. The flowers are attractive to bees.

Winter Tare (*Vicia sativa*) A hardy annual growing to 75 cm (30 in) tall and exceptionally hardy. This is a fast-growing bushy vetch which provides plenty of weed-smothering leaf cover. It is nitrogen-fixing, dislikes drought and prefers alkaline soils. Plant in summer or autumn to overwinter. Reasonably easy to dig in.

A FEW TIPS ON GREEN MANURING

+ Prepare the ground as well for green manures as for any other crop. If your soil is poor, apply a general fertilizer like blood fish and bone first.

+ Small seeds can be broadcast on prepared soil and raked in. Large seed is usually sown in drills about 30 cm (1 ft) apart each way.

+ Low-growing crops are chopped up with a spade. Large plants can be broken down by mowing, scything or strimming. Plants are left to wilt on the surface for a few days before being dug in.

+ For maximum benefit bury green manures no deeper than 15 cm (6 in).

+ If you have let the crop get woody, a dousing of liquid animal manure (see page 30) will help it to rot down more quickly.

CHAPTER

4_

clever
tricks
and cunning
plans

Now the basics are all in place, you can juggle with the plantings to make the most of your land by intercropping, under cropping, catch cropping and strip cropping. With the use of temperature charts and crop covers, and by choosing your varieties wisely, you can cheat the weather a little, keeping summer crops until December, enjoying the earliest spring ones and having salad greens growing right through winter.

PROVIDING COVER

The best possible way to grow plants is to work hand in hand with nature. This means sowing and growing at the optimum time for the individual plants and giving them the ideal conditions for their particular needs. The aim is to grow them to maturity quickly to avoid trouble, any 'checking', or hitches in the natural progression that might set them back or weaken them. Trying to grow vegetables out of season is to go against the grain and makes extra work and increased cost for the grower.

This said, sometimes just a few degrees of easily provided extra warmth can give you a bonus of time and flexibility. There is a

good idea

Another trick to get ahead is to pre-warm the soil by covering it with black polythene for a couple of weeks before you plan to sow your seed. In this way you can move most of the categories up (or half way up) into the next section.

cut-off point for most plants. For most hardy cool season vegetables the soil temperature needs to be around 4–7°C (40–45°F) for germination. When the temperature drops below this in autumn the plants will cease to grow. Cool season crops need a cool period prior to the warmth of summer to grow well.

By using crop covers (anything from a cold greenhouse, a cold frame, a cloche, polythene, netting or fleece) you can fairly effortlessly raise the temperature to above the cut-off point and so extend the season at each end. With cover and a little luck, you can keep your lettuces growing until Christmas and enjoy earliest spring peas and carrots.

With cover you can keep some vegetables – the hardier types of lettuces, celtuce, corn salad, rocket, Florence fennel, endive, mizuna and mibuna greens – ticking over right through winter. Tender vegetables that might otherwise fail to prosper outdoors in a British spring, such as dwarf and runner beans, can be sown or

MINIMUM TEMPERATURES

These are the minimum average daytime temperatures needed for active growth of the following crops:

4°C (40°F)
Artichoke
Beet
Broad bean
Broccoli
Brussels sprouts
Cabbage
Cardoon
Carrot
Cauliflower
Celeriac
Celery
Chard
Florence fennel
Kale
Kohlrabi
Lettuce
Mustard leaves
Parsley
Parsnip
Peas
Potatoes
Radish
Spinach
Turnip

7°C (45°F)
Chicory
Garlic
Leek
Onion
Salsify
Scorzonera
Shallot

10°C (50°F)
New Zealand spinach
Pumpkin
Squash
Sweetcorn

15°C (59°F)
Cucumber

18°C (64°F)
Aubergine
Capsicum
Chilli
Okra
Sweet potato
Tomato

planted outside in chilly April and kept warm under cloches until all danger of frost has passed in late May.

VEGETABLES HARDY TO −5°C (23°F)

(providing the soil is free draining)
American land cress
Asparagus
Burdock
Broad beans (winter varieties)
Broccoli (perennial)
Brussels sprouts
Cabbage (winter varieties)
Calabrese
Cardoon
Chicory
Chinese artichokes
Chives
Cauliflowers (winter varieties)
Celery, trench (winter varieties)
Garlic (needs a period of cold)
Globe artichoke (except in waterlogged soils)
Hamburg parsley
Horseradish
Good King Henry
Jerusalem artichokes
Kale (winter varieties)
Kohlrabi
Komatsuna
Leek

Mustards (winter varieties)
Onions (winter varieties)
Onions, Japanese (they need to be 15–20 cm (6–8 in) tall by the first frosts)
Onions, Japanese bunching
Spring onions (winter varieties)
Onions, Welsh
Orache
Pak choi (winter varieties, under cover)
Parsley (under cover)
Parsnip (improves with the frost)
Peas (winter varieties)
Quinoa
Radish
Rhubarb
Rocket (under cover)
Salsify
Scorzonera
Seakale
Spinach (winter varieties)
Spinach beet
Sprouting broccoli
Swede
Texcel greens
Turnip

Cool- and warm-season vegetables

Vegetables are generally divided into two broad groups. With a few exceptions (such as peas and broad beans), cool-season types are grown for their edible roots, stems, leaves, buds or immature flowers. They germinate at low temperatures and can take some frost, either being fully hardy or half-hardy. They are less vigorous than the warm-season counterparts and have shallower

HALF-HARDY VEGETABLES

Asparagus pea
Beetroot (can survive a mild winter)
Carrot
Cauliflower (winter varieties)
Celeriac (can be left out in mild areas through winter)
Celery
Celtuce (under cover)
Chard (best under cover)
Chicory
Chinese broccoli (can take some frost after the seedling stage)
Chinese cabbage
Corn salad (under cover)

Florence fennel (can take a little cold)
Globe artichoke
Endive (under cover)
Lettuce (depending on variety, can be grown through winter under cover)
Mizuna and mibuna greens (can take most winters under cover)
Onions, bulb
Onions, globe
Parsnip
Potato
Radiccio
Salsify
Shallots

TENDER VEGETABLES

Amaranthus
Chrysanthemum greens
Celery (self-blanching and summer types)
Courgettes (and marrows)
French beans
New Zealand spinach

Runner beans
Snap bean
Soy bean
Squash (summer and winter varieties)
Sweetcorn
Tomato

VERY TENDER VEGETABLES

Aubergine
Chilli
Cucumber
Lablab bean
Lima bean
Melon

Okra
Pepper
Pumpkin
Sweet potato
Watermelon
Yard long bean

roots. The softer, more luxuriant, warm-season vegetables (with the exception of sweet potato and New Zealand spinach) are grown for their fruits, both sweet and savoury.

Types of crop cover

The cold frame is invaluable for raising cool-weather crops from seed in autumn and spring, for hardening off those raised indoors and for holding young seedlings before they are planted out if the weather deteriorates. It is also a good place to grow crops through winter. People skilled in DIY can easily knock one up. The most basic sort can be constructed from an old drawer with a glass or clear plastic top. It is important that the top can be easily removed for watering and preventing plants scorching on hot days.

Cold frames should be sited to face south and ideally have a sloping roof to get maximum sunshine. Some gardeners sink the base slightly into the soil for additional warmth in winter. In really cold weather, they can be covered at night with sacks or old blankets and bales of straw can be leant against them.

As soon as the temperature goes above 7°C (45°F), the top should be slightly raised to let in air but closed again at night. Watering should be done in the morning so that the plants are dry by night to avoid too much humidity and the danger of damping off and disease.

Fleece is a fine, light-as-air, non-abrasive fabric made of spun bonded polypropylene or polyester. It is ultraviolet (UV) resistant. The primary benefit is that it raises the temperature by some three or four degrees at night and about ten degrees during the day. It is said to protect against frost down to −5°C (23°F). Rain and air pass through it easily.

Fleece also protects plants against flying pests – though it's important to get the right mesh size to target the particular pest. There are various grades varying from summer to winter weights. It comes made into drawstring bags that can be used over individual plants. Generally, however, fleece is used as a 'floating' mulch, covering an entire crop, sometimes for the duration of the growing period. It is put over loosely to allow for growth and held down all round with weights and a ridge of soil. A few crops, particularly tomatoes, squashes and peppers, need hoops to prevent the netting touching the fruits. If handled with care to avoid tearing, fleece can last several years.

Enviromesh is the wonder mesh that has transformed organic husbandry. It is particularly useful for young seedlings as a physical barrier against onion fly, pea moth, cutworm, cabbage whitefly, leaf miners, butterflies and aphids. It takes the edge off wind and heavy rain, and gives a degree of frost protection. It is expected to last eight to ten years.

Polytunnels Some allotments don't allow anything larger than a mini polytunnel as they consider larger ones to be a blot on the landscape. Another worry is that any large, possibly permanent,

DID YOU KNOW?

The principle of strip cropping is to grow crops that need protection at different times of the year in parallel rows. The cloches can then be moved with minimum effort from one row to the next and back again (see page 77). This takes a little planning, but it is an economic way to maximize both the use of the cloches and the space. It allows you to maximize one small area.

feature could create a problem for the next tenant. Battles have been won with the argument that a free-standing polytunnel can be moved around the plot (at least technically speaking) and so it is a moveable structure like a giant cloche and unlikely to be left behind like a greenhouse or a tree. Another argument you can put forward is that cloches conserve water. Some allotment committees draw a line on size, allowing polytunnels no larger than 2.4 x 3 m (8 x 10 ft), their maximum green house size, while others put a restriction on anything larger than 25 per cent of the area of the plot.

A STRIP CROPPING PROGRAMME

Plants fall into three or four main groups for cloching.

Group 1 Sow in July or August, cloche late September or early October, clear either in November or in spring.

✦ Chinese cabbage

✦ Endive

✦ Lettuce, autumn

✦ Peas

Group 2 Sow in October, January or February and keep under cloches until April or May.

✦ American landcress

✦ Broad beans (sow in January or February)

✦ Spring cabbage (cloche in early spring for an early crop)

✦ Calabrese (sow in late autumn)

✦ Carrots (sow in September or February in mild areas)

✦ Cauliflower

✦ Celtuce

✦ Chard

✦ Chinese broccoli (sow in early autumn)

✦ Chicory (sugarloaf and Witloof types for blanching)

✦ Corn salad

✦ Endive (Batavian types)

✦ Good King Henry

✦ Kohlrabi (sow in February in mild areas when temperature is over 10°C (50°F) – not without risk)

✦ Komatsuna (sow in autumn)

✦ Lettuce (hardy varieties)

✦ Mibuna and mizuna greens (sow in autumn for winter use)

✦ Pak choi (hardy varieties, sow in autumn)

✦ Peas (earlies)

✦ Potatoes (earlies)

✦ Rocket

✦ Spinach (winter varieties, sow in August)

✦ Spinach beet (sow in mid to late summer)

A STRIP CROPPING PROGRAMME

Group 3 Sow in April or May and keep under cloches for a few weeks until the end of the frosts in early June.

✦ Broad beans

✦ Brussels sprouts (earlies)

✦ Cabbage (summer)

✦ French beans

✦ Pak choi (seedling crop)

✦ Peas (maincrop varieties)

✦ Runner beans

✦ Swedes

✦ Turnips (earlies)

Group 4 Tender plants planted out in April or May under cloches and can remain under them until they are cleared at the end of September. These are grown from seed with heat or bought as small plants.

✦ Aubergine

✦ Chillies

✦ Cucumbers

✦ Gherkin

✦ Lablab Beans

✦ Melons

✦ Okra

✦ Peppers

✦ Squashes

✦ Sweet Potato

✦ Sweetcorn

✦ Tomatoes

Cloches The cloche is a lightweight portable structure. The Victorian version was a glass bell-shaped plant cover. You can buy plastic copies though the ingenious allotment version that works just as well is a big plastic water bottle with the bottom sawn off and screw top removed for air circulation. The 'barn' type, aimed to cover a row of plants, is usually standard in length and width but varying in height to suit different crops.

Portable mini tunnel cloches come made from UV-stabilized polythene or covered in fleece or netting. Net tunnel cloches made from polyethylene netting are handy for protecting crops like strawberries from birds and insects, and protecting plants from scorching. A standard size is 3 m (10 ft) in length, 45 cm (18 in) wide and 30 cm (12 in) high. Some will concertina down for storage.

You can get 'self-watering' cloches in the same material with gutters to direct rainwater back into the soil. There are also rigid mini polytunnels made from corrugated UV-stabilized plastic.

Intensive growing under cover

✦ If the soil is expected to perform non-stop, it is important to build up the fertility and to keep it high by incorporating plenty of well-rotted manure or compost. You may need to give the plants an additional boost with a fertilizer such as blood, fish and bone from time to time.

✦ Improving the texture of the soil with organic matter and using mulches on top will help the soil to retain moisture. This is important as most of the rainwater sinks down vertically each side of the cloches and only about 10 per cent will percolate sideways to the plant roots.

✦ If the soil is cold, cover it with black polythene for a few days to warm it up before sowing.

✦ If you are making a row of cloches, make sure that the ground is flat and use a line to align them.

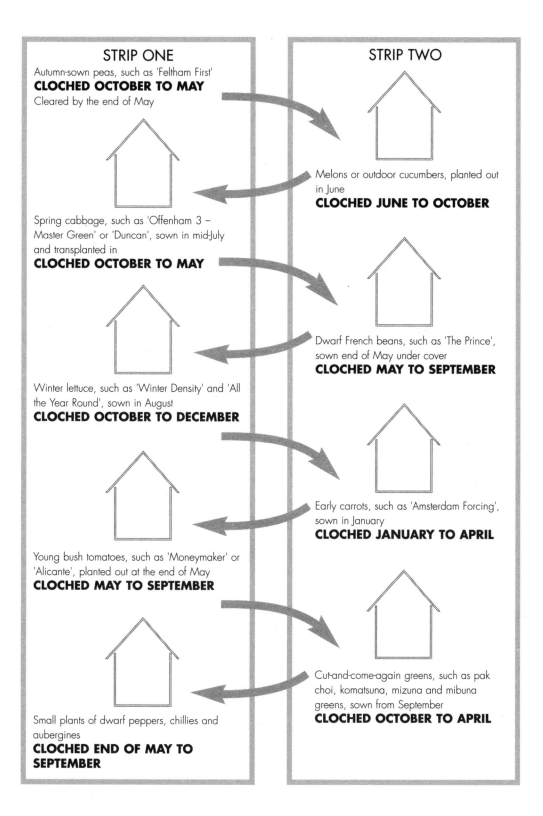

STRIP ONE

Autumn-sown peas, such as 'Feltham First'
CLOCHED OCTOBER TO MAY
Cleared by the end of May

Spring cabbage, such as 'Offenham 3 –
Master Green' or 'Duncan', sown in mid-July
and transplanted in
CLOCHED OCTOBER TO MAY

Winter lettuce, such as 'Winter Density' and 'All
the Year Round', sown in August
CLOCHED OCTOBER TO DECEMBER

Young bush tomatoes, such as 'Moneymaker' or
'Alicante', planted out at the end of May
CLOCHED MAY TO SEPTEMBER

Small plants of dwarf peppers, chillies and
aubergines
**CLOCHED END OF MAY TO
SEPTEMBER**

STRIP TWO

Melons or outdoor cucumbers, planted out
in June
CLOCHED JUNE TO OCTOBER

Dwarf French beans, such as 'The Prince',
sown end of May under cover
CLOCHED MAY TO SEPTEMBER

Early carrots, such as 'Amsterdam Forcing',
sown in January
CLOCHED JANUARY TO APRIL

Cut-and-come-again greens, such as pak
choi, komatsuna, mizuna and mibuna
greens, sown from September
CLOCHED OCTOBER TO APRIL

+ If the soil is very wet, cloche it for several days.

+ As you will want to catch the maximum heat in winter, make sure that the glass or plastic is clean. In summer, traditionally the cloches would be whitewashed to avoid scorching.

A few ideas for strip cropping under cover

As nothing in nature works entirely to schedule, it is as well to use common sense, take account of your own weather and leave a margin for the unexpected. With a little thought you can maintain the rotation system under cover, leaving out potatoes as they don't need protection.

You can follow legumes with brassicas, like spring cabbage, early cauliflower or cut-and-come-again greens – and brassicas with root vegetables. You can give the soil a break with tender 'fruiting' vegetables like tomatoes or peppers in the summer.

In among the main crops, you can always slot in radishes, lettuce, salad onions and salad greens and other cut-and-come-again mixtures. The main thing is not to overdo one family of vegetables in the same soil year after year. Some people avoid any possibility of trouble by replacing the existing soil with fresh soil from another part of the allotment each year – not too arduous a task as it is only over a small area.

Traditional practices

The Victorians were masters of growing out of season. In large estates they would grow all the exotics, even bananas and pineapples, in heated greenhouses. An under lad whose job was to stoke the boilers throughout the night would be on hand sleeping in a bed in the hayloft or shed nearby. They also cleverly devised the hotbed – a way to provide heat with little more than fresh manure for seedlings to grow out of season. A simpler way to relieve the boredom of winter vegetables in the 'hungry gap' of late winter was by forcing.

Forcing without heat

In mild areas, Witloof chicory can be blanched outside. Cut the leaves down to 5 cm (2 in) in autumn and cover the entire plant with straw, leafmould or soil, then put a bucket on top, or a flowerpot with the holes blocked to cut out any light.

Alternatively, dig up the plants in late autumn or early winter, cut the leaves off as before and trim the roots to 30 cm (12 in). Store them in moist sand in a frost-free shed. When you want to grow them on, plant them in large pots of moist compost with the crowns just showing. Keep in the dark at a minimum of 10°C (50°F). The chicons will grow within a month.

Wild seakale, blanched under sand, was considered a great delicacy in the 19th century and deserves to be reinstated. A herbaceous perennial, seakale is usually grown from offsets or 'thongs', though you can buy the seed as well. In the autumn, cut away all the dying foliage from the plants. In February or March, cover the crowns with a forcing pot, a bucket or bin, or a frame covered with black polythene. Alternatively, cover the plants with leafmould or sand. The same technique can be used with rhubarb.

THE HOTBED

The hotbed is an energy free way of getting your plants going with bottom heat. Victorian gardeners used them for out-of-season crops. The basic essential is a good pile of fresh manure mixed in with straw bedding. You also need a cold frame lid or cloche and a soil thermometer. The bigger the heap the hotter you can get it to be. You would need a heap about 1.2 m (4 ft) square to get a temperature of around 27°C (80°F) but you can get helpful heat from a much smaller pile. For the first week turn the heap over once or twice a day, to mix it. You can either build the heap on the ground or build it in a pit around 30 cm (12 in) deep. The pit gives it more insulation on light soils but on cold clay it would be better to build it on the surface. Make a neat square heap that is rock stable with a flat top for the cover. Bash it down to compact it. Leave it for a few more days to settle and for any steam to escape. Finally, check the temperature. If it is 24°C (80°F) or over, let it cool for another couple of days. Layer on 10 cm (4 in) of topsoil and sow into this. Cover with the cloche top leaving a few chinks for steam to escape.

MAXIMIZING THE SPACE

You may feel that you have endless space on your allotment so why waste your energy and resources bringing the soil in all ten poles up to scratch? You can work on tiers of fertility, with the top tier being the borders for the annual vegetables, the middle tier for perennials, herbs and flowers, and the bottom tier being zero work on the paths.

Vegetable planting distances

The standard plant spacings are worked out with maximum yield in mind. The idea is to give each plant enough room to grow comfortably without competition from its neighbour. Other considerations are to space them close enough together to keep down weeds by providing

STANDARD SPACINGS AFTER THINNING FOR FULL-SIZED CROPS

	PLANT SPACING	ROW SPACING
Artichoke, globe	75 cm (30 in)	90 cm (3 ft)
Artichoke, Jerusalem	30 cm (12 in)	30 cm (12 in)
Artichoke, Chinese	15–30 cm (6–12 in)	45 cm (18 in)
Asparagus	15 cm (6 in)	30 cm (12 in)
Aubergine	60–75 cm (24–30 in)	75–90 cm (30–36 in)
Beetroot (early)	10 cm (4 in)	23 cm (9 in)
Broad beans (double rows)	23 cm (9 in)	23 cm (9 in), 60 cm (24 in) between each set
Broad bean (single rows)	23 cm (9 in)	45 cm (18 in)
Beetroot (maincrop)	7.5 cm (3 in)	30 cm (12 in)
Broccoli, sprouting	60 cm (24 in)	60 cm (24 in)
Brussels sprouts (short)	45 cm (18 in)	45 cm (18 in)
Brussels sprouts (tall)	60–90 cm (24–36 in)	45 cm (18 in)
Cabbage (spring)	25 cm (10 in)	30 cm (12 in)
Cabbage (summer)	38 cm (15 in)	38 cm (15 in)
Cabbage (autumn and winter)	45 cm (18 in)	45 cm (18 in)
Cabbage, red	30 cm (12 in)	45 cm (18 in)

STANDARD SPACINGS AFTER THINNING FOR FULL-SIZED CROPS

	PLANT SPACING	ROW SPACING
Calabrese	30 cm (12 in)	45 cm (18 in)
Cardoon	38 cm (15 in)	45 cm (18 in)
Carrots (early)	7.5 cm (3 in)	15 cm (6 in)
Carrots (maincrop)	4 cm (1 1/2 in)	15 cm (6 in)
Cauliflower (summer)	45 cm (18 in)	60 cm (24 in)
Cauliflower (autumn)	60 cm (24 in)	60 cm (24 in)
Cauliflower (winter)	70 cm (28 in)	70 cm (28 in)
Celeriac	30 cm (12 in)	45 cm (18 in)
Celery (trench)	30–45 cm (12–18 in)	30 cm (12 in)
Celery (self-blanching)	25 cm (10 in)	25 cm (10 in)
Celtuce	10 cm (4 in)	30 cm (12 in)
Chicory (witloof)	23 cm (9 in)	30 cm (12 in)
Chicory (sugarloaf)	30 cm (12 in)	30 cm (12 in)
Chicory (radiccio)	30 cm (12 in)	30 cm (12 in)
Chilli	38–45 cm (15–18 in)	60–75 cm (24–30 in)
Chinese broccoli	30 cm (12 in)	30 cm (12 in)
Chinese cabbage	30 cm (12 in)	45 cm (18 in)
Courgette (bush)	90 cm (3 ft)	90 cm (3 ft)
Courgette (trailing)	90 cm (3 ft)	1.2 m (4 ft)
Cucumber (outdoor on the flat)	60–75 cm (24–30 in)	1.5 m (5 ft)
Cucumber (trained)	45 cm (18 in)	1 m (3 ft 4 in)
Endive	23 cm (9 in)	30 cm (12 in)
Florence fennel	30 cm (12 in)	30 cm (12 in)
French bean (dwarf)	5–7.5 cm (2–3 in)	45–60 cm (18–24 in)
French beans (climbing single rows)	5–7.5 cm (2–3 in)	45 cm (18 in)
French beans (climbing double rows)	15 cm (6 in)	23 cm (9 in), 60 cm (24 in)
Garlic	18 cm (7 in)	30 cm (12 in)
Hamburg parsley	15–20 cm (6–8 in)	30 cm (12 in)
Kale (short)	30–45 cm (12–18 in)	45 cm (18 in)
Kale (tall)	60 cm (24 in)	45–60 cm (18–24 in)
Kohlrabi	23 cm (9 in)	30 cm (12 in)
Komatsuna	2.5 cm (1 in)	45 cm (18 in)
Mizuna and mibuna greens	45 cm (18 in)	23 cm (9 in)
Leek	15–20 cm (6–8 in)	30–38 cm (12–15 in)

STANDARD SPACINGS AFTER THINNING FOR FULL-SIZED CROPS

	PLANT SPACING	ROW SPACING
Lettuce	35 cm (14 in)	38 cm (15 in)
Lettuce, butterhead	25 cm (10 in)	30 cm (12 in)
Marrow (bush)	90 cm (3 ft)	90 cm (3 ft)
Marrow (trailing)	90 cm (3 ft)	1.2 m (4 ft)
Mustard greens	15–30 cm (6–12 in)	45 cm (18 in)
Okra	40–60 cm (16–24 in)	60–75 cm (24–30 in)
Onions, bulb	5–10 cm (2–4 in)	30 cm (12 in)
Onions, Japanese bunching	7.5 cm (3 in)	30 cm (12 in)
Onions, globe	5–10 cm (2–4 in)	30 cm (12 in)
Onions, pickling	0.5 cm ($^1/_4$ in)	30 cm (12 in)
Onions, spring	1 cm ($^1/_2$ in)	30 cm (12 in)
Onions, Welsh	20 cm (8 in)	23 cm (9 in)
Pak choi	10 cm (4 in)	45 cm (18 in)
Parsnip	15 cm (6 in)	30 cm (12 in)
Peas	7.5 cm (3 in)	30–60 cm (12–24 in)
Peppers (sweet)	38–45 cm (15–18 in)	60–75 cm (24–30 in)
Potato (early)	30–38 cm (12–15 in)	38–50 cm (15–20 in)
Potatoes (second early)	35–45 cm (14–18 in)	65–75 cm (25–30 in)
Potatoes (maincrop)	35–45 cm (14–18 in)	65–75 cm (25–30 in)
Pumpkin (bush)	90 cm (3 ft)	90 cm (3 ft)
Pumpkin (trailing)	1.5 m (5 ft)	1.5 m (5 ft)
Radish, mooli	23 cm (9 in)	30 cm (12 in)
Radish, salad	1 cm ($^1/_2$ in)	15 cm (6 in)
Radish, winter	23 cm (9 in)	30 cm (12 in)
Rhubarb	75–90 cm (30–36 in)	30 cm (12 in)
Rocket	15 cm (6 in)	15 cm (6 in)
Runner beans (double rows)	15 cm (6 in)	60 cm (24 in), 1.5 m (5 ft) between each set
Runner beans (dwarf)	15 cm (6 in)	45 cm (18 in)
Salsify	10 cm (4 in)	15–30 cm (6–12 in)
Scorzonera	10 cm (4 in)	15–30 cm (6–12 in)
Seakale	38 cm (15 in)	38 cm (15 in)
Shallot	15–20 cm (6–8 in)	30 cm (12 in)

STANDARD SPACINGS AFTER THINNING FOR FULL-SIZED CROPS		
	PLANT SPACING	**ROW SPACING**
Squash (summer bush)	90 cm (3 ft)	90 cm (3 ft)
Squash (summer trailing)	90 cm (3 ft)	1.5 m (5 ft)
Squash (winter)	1.2–1.8 m (4–6 ft)	1.2–1.5 m (4–5 ft)
Spinach	15 cm (6 in)	30 cm (12 in)
Spinach (New Zealand)	45 cm (18 in)	45 cm (18 in)
Spinach beet	20 cm (8 in)	45 cm (18 in)
Strawberry	30 cm (12 in)	30 cm (12 in)
Summer purslane	15 cm (6 in)	15 cm (6 in)
Swede	23 cm (9 in)	38 cm (15 in)
Sweetcorn	35–45 cm (14–18 in)	45–60 cm (18–24 in)
Swiss chard	20 cm (8 in)	45 cm (18 in)
Sweet potato	25–30 cm (10–12 in)	75 cm (30 in)
Tomatillo	45 cm (18 in)	90 cm (3 ft)
Tomato (bush)	30–90 cm (1–3 ft)	90 cm (3 ft)
Tomato (vine)	38–45 cm (15–18 in)	90 cm (3 ft)
Texcel greens	2.5 cm (1 in)	30 cm (12 in)
Turnip (early)	10 cm (4 in)	23 cm (9 in)
Turnip (maincrop)	15 cm (6 in)	30 cm (12 in)
Winter purslane	15 cm (6 in)	23 cm (9 in)

uninterrupted leaf cover. On the other hand, where you are growing plants like onions with narrow leaves that can't shade out weeds, it is perhaps better to space them wider apart than recommended so that you can hoe around them with ease. Generally speaking, the spacings increase as you go forward into the growing season, with maincrop varieties being generally larger and needing more space than earlies. Deciding on the amount of plants ('the population') and their arrangement ('the pattern') is one area of gardening over which we have control. However, within a single packet, some seed will come up early and be vigorous, while others may fail to thrive. F1 hybrids are more uniform, however, although the seed is more expensive.

Controlling the size of vegetables

While traditional gardeners are inclined to think that big is beautiful, consumers often prefer smaller vegetables. They are more appetizing if young, tender and sweet. 'Baby' vegetables are considered to be desirable both for their appearance and taste and are more expensive in the shops than normal-sized ones. Most seed catalogues have a section of 'mini veg' and these are dwarf cultivars. However, some vegetables can be grown to be small simply by planting them closer together than is normally recommended.

Onions are a classic example. If you want large onions you space them 10 cm (4 in) apart, and if you want medium-sized ones you halve the distance. Leeks respond brilliantly to the same treatment. Whereas there is a limit for most vegetables beyond which you will deprive the plant, with leeks you can cut the planting distance down dramatically from the normal 15–20 cm (6–8 in) right down to a tenth of that – 1.5 cm (3/4 in).

For small parsnips, reduce the spacing down from 15 cm (6 in) to 10 cm (4 in). When it comes to the ever-adaptable oriental vegetables, the spacing depends on whether you want to grow them as cut-and-come-again, or to semi or full maturity.

Carrots are exceptional in being ready to eat throughout their entire growth – even the smallest thinnings are good in salads. The clever gardener might decide to space crops according to his or her individual needs with a proportion of both small and large vegetables to meet every occasion.

Planting patterns

Planting in straight rows comes directly from the horse-drawn plough and the mechanized seed drill. There is little reason to sow in rows if you are sowing by hand, apart from the fact that if you sow north to south you will get an even distribution of sunshine. The sun shines from the east in the morning, from the south midday, or overhead in summer, and from the west in the afternoon.

If plants are too close together the leaves will shade each other.

Straight rows with a gap leave room for weeds.

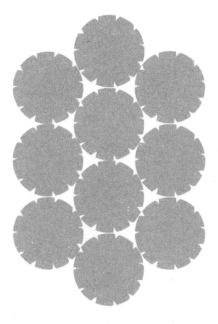

Blocks in this pattern make maximum use of space.

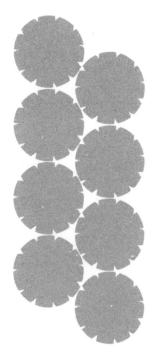

Staggered rows make better use of space.

SOME RESULTS OF TRIALS OF CLOSE PLANTING

The following results come from research by The National Vegetable Research Station.

Summer cabbage Spaced at the lower end of the recommended planting distance of 35 cm (14 in), summer cabbages gave the highest yield of small heads. At the wider spacing of 45 cm (18 in) the heads were bigger and earlier hearting, but there was 65 per cent less cabbage in the same space.

Calabrese Trials with calabrese planted at different distances resulted in similar yields. Those planted more closely in 'higher populations', spaced 15 x 30 cm (6 x12 in), came out with half the yield from the top shoots and half from the side shoots. The widest spacings resulted in the largest spears and most plentiful side shoots. The closest spacings prevented the side shoots growing very much and resulted in smaller terminal (topmost) spears ready for harvesting at the same time. This is ideal for commercial growers who want to harvest in one swoop and get onto the next crop, but perhaps of less interest to the allotment holder with a family to feed.

Tomatoes Experiments of cutting the spacing of outdoor bush tomatoes from 0.5 sq m (0.5 sq yd) by half resulted in much the same total yield by the end of the season, but with more tomatoes early in the season when they are expensive in the shops, and less at the end, when there is usually a glut.

Potatoes Potatoes respond to the space that they are given – the more space they have, the more prolific they will be and the bigger the tubers. However, large tubers with lots of 'eyes' can become overcrowded and entangled causing 'clumping'. This forces the tubers up to the surface, causing 'greening' (poisonous green patches to form) unless you are quick with the earthing-up. You can avoid both clumping and earthing-up altogether and get the highest yields by planting more small seed potatoes with less 'eyes' (growing buds).

A geometric pattern to your seed drills is desirable as you can instantly differentiate between weed and seed, but it needn't be a straight line.

The aim should be to cover the ground with foliage to black out the weeds, without the leaves of your plants overlapping each other.

INTERCROPPING

Intercropping is the art of taking advantage of planting gaps in various ways. It is using the temporary spaces between slow-growing plants like Brussels sprouts. As they won't need the full space allotted to them for many weeks, a quick crop of lettuce or radish can be grown in between the small Brussels sprouts plants.

The golden rule is to put the needs of the slow grower, or the host, first. Occasionally you may even need to sacrifice the intercrop if it is taking too much space or nutrients needed by the main crop. Plant in the middle of the gap and err on the cautious side. It is important to keep the soil in excellent condition by feeding it with plenty of muck and mulch.

Host plants

The following are slow growers or plants that crop over a long time:

+ Brussels sprouts: 5 months
+ Cabbage (summer and autumn types): 4–6 months
+ Carrots (maincrop): 5 months
+ Cauliflower (summer and autumn types): 16 weeks
+ Cauliflower (winter types): 10 months
+ Celery (trench celery): 9 months
+ Garlic (from bulbs): 4–9 months
+ Leeks: 4–5 months
+ Onions (spring-planted sets): $4^1/_2$–5 months
+ Parsnips: 4 months
+ Salsify: 4–5 months

Fast-growing plants

+ Amaranthus: 10–12 weeks
+ Carrot (earlies): 9 weeks
+ Chard: 8–12 weeks
+ Chinese broccoli: 10 weeks
+ Chinese cabbage: 8–10 weeks
+ Chrysanthemum greens: 8–10 weeks
+ Endive: 7–13 weeks
+ Japanese bunching onion: 8 weeks for salad onions
+ Kohlrabi: 5–9 weeks
+ Komatsuna: 7 weeks in summer
+ Lettuce: 4–6 weeks, depending on variety

+ Mizuna and mibuna greens:
  6–8 weeks to semi-maturity,
  8–10 to maturity
+ Mustard greens: 6–8 weeks
+ Pak choi: 8 weeks
+ Squash (summer): 7–8 weeks
+ Radish (salad): 4 weeks
+ Radish (mooli): 8 weeks in the
  growing season
+ Rocket: 4–12 weeks
+ Spinach: 5–10 weeks
+ Summer purslane: 4–12 weeks
+ Turnips (earlies): 5 weeks
+ Turnips (maincrop):
  6–10 weeks

Underplanting

Another form of intercropping is
to grow low shade-loving plants
under tall plants – filling a
vertical gap. Leafy greens are
ideal for the underplanting as the
leaves will grow ever bigger to
absorb more light. If you plant
lettuce with young sweetcorn, it
will have full sun in the early
summer and desirable semi-shade
in the heat of midsummer.

Tall hosts for intercropping

+ Artichoke, globe
+ Beans, French
+ Beans, Runner
+ Cardoons
+ Courgettes (growing on
  supports)
+ Cucumbers, trailing (growing on
  supports)
+ Orache
+ Peas
+ Squashes (growing on supports)
+ Sunflowers
+ Tomatoes

Short plants for undercropping

+ American landcress
+ Celtuce
+ Chicory
+ Chinese cabbage
+ Chrysanthemum greens
+ Corn salad
+ Endive
+ Good King Henry
+ Lettuce
+ Pak choi
+ Parsley
+ Spinach
+ Texcel greens

Narrow plants for intercropping
+ Brussels sprouts
+ Carrots
+ Celery
+ Garlic
+ Leeks
+ Onions
+ Sweetcorn

Short and wide plants for intercropping
+ Cabbage
+ Cauliflower
+ Chicory
+ Chinese cabbage
+ Corn salad
+ Endive
+ Florence fennel
+ Kohlrabi
+ Lettuce
+ Mibuna greens
+ Mizuna greens
+ Pak choi
+ Parsnips
+ Rocket
+ Radiccio

Catch cropping
Fast growers that will be out before the maincrop needs the space.

+ Any cut-and-come-again
+ Amaranthus
+ Chinese cabbage (from 3 weeks)
+ Corn salad
+ Endive (curly)
+ Good King Henry
+ Lettuce (cutting types such as 'Salad Bowl')
+ Mizuna and mibuna greens (2–3 weeks)
+ Mustard (red)
+ Orache
+ Pak choi
+ Purslane (summer)
+ Rocket
+ Spinach
+ Texcel greens

MIXED SOWINGS

The shops are full of interesting *Mesclun* and *Misticanza* – mixes of 'French', 'Italian', 'American', 'baby leaf', 'herb' and 'spicy' salad leaves as well as 'Oriental saladini'. You can purchase ready mixed seed or, even better, why not create your own favourite mixes for a fraction of the cost? The way to get a non-stop succession is to sow a few seeds every week, starting in spring under crop covers, carrying on right through summer and sowing hardier varieties under crop covers from September for winter eating.

Most lettuces grow about 15 cm (6 in), ready to cut in 35–40 days, depending on the season. When cutting the leaves, always leave about 2.5–5 cm (1–2 in) of stump so that more leaves will grow. Lettuces, as well as all the other types of salad greens, will re-sprout two or three times before running out of steam.

With this much production, it is important to keep soil fertility high. Incorporate well-rotted manure into the soil before you start and keep the plants well fertilized. Although the types of brassicas used in this way grow so fast that they will probably avoid clubroot, it is good practice to rotate them with the other crops.

Young green leaves for salads and stir-fries

Amaranthus, calaloo or Indian spinach (*Amaranthus gangeticus*) is a classic cooked with salt fish in Jamaican cuisine. It is not hardy and needs a warm sheltered site. A very fast grower, it germinates within two weeks and lasts 2–3 months in summer.

American landcress (*Barbarea vulgaris*) is much like watercress in appearance and its peppery taste but, unlike it, is easy to grow given a moist shady spot. Sow seed in August to harvest through winter.

Chrysanthemum greens (*Chrysanthemum coronarium*) are much enjoyed by the Japanese. The young leaves are picked when no bigger than 10 cm (4 in). The best time to sow is in late summer up to the frosts.

Good King Henry (*Cheonopodium bonus-henricus*) is an easy plant, not found in the shops as it wilts quickly after picking. A perennial with decorative leaves, you can cut off the leaves the first spring after it is sown. For maximum cropping, divide it each spring.

Lambs lettuce, corn salad or mâche (*Valerianella locusta*) is a classic in the 'French' mix, and best sown after midsummer to avoid bolting. After that sow every two weeks with cover over winter.

Loose-leaved lettuce The best cut-and-come-again lettuces are the loose-leaved types, in the categories of the oak leaf, the wavy leafed 'Salad Bowl, 'Lollo Rossa', 'Lollo Bionda' and the brightly coloured 'Can Can'. The seed is fine so mix it with a little sand. Try to sow no less than about 2.5 cm (1 in) apart. Keep well watered. They need dappled shade in summer.

Mizuna and mibuna greens (*Brassica rapa* and *B.r. nipposinica*) produce pretty, healthy-looking spoon-shaped or raggedy leaves for salads when young, and are good for stir-fries when bigger. Sow mizuna in spring or late summer, mibuna in late summer only. They grow so fast that they need to be cut almost every day.

Orache (*Atriplex hortensis*) is very colourful, with claret, gold and green-leafed varieties. It grows like a weed from spring onwards but usually goes to seed by midsummer.

Pak choi (*Brassica rapa* var. *chinensis*) is delicious in stir-fries and salads when young. It needs care to grow well. Sow under cover in spring and in July for an autumn harvest.

Rocket (*Eruca sativa*), the gourmet mustard-tasting leaf, is hardy, easy, and can be grown right round the year given some protection in winter.

Spinach (*Spinacea oleracea*) grows best in the cool conditions of spring, and autumn for the following spring. Use the young leaves for salads and let the plants grow on for cooked greens.

GOURMET SALADS AND STIR-FRIES
MARCH TO AUGUST

	MARCH	APRIL	MAY	JUNE	JULY	AUGUST
Rocket	SOW					
Good King Henry		SOW				
Orache		SOW				
Spinach		SOW				SOW
Mizuna greens		SOW				SOW
Texcel greens		SOW				
Loose-leaved lettuce		SOW				SOW
Pak choi		SOW				SOW
Amaranthus			SOW			
Chrysanthemum greens					SOW	
American landcress						SOW
Mibuna greens						SOW
Lamb's lettuce						SOW

Texcel greens (*Brassica carinata*) are the new wonder fast-growing green, great for catch crops. Young leaves are a spicy addition to salads or stir-fries or they can be grown on and cooked like spinach. Don't let them grow too big, however, or they will coarsen. Grow from seed in spring onwards and through winter under crop covers.

GOURMET SALADS AND STIR-FRIES
SEPTEMBER TO FEBRUARY

	SEPTEMBER	OCTOBER	NOVEMBER	DECEMBER	JANUARY	FEBRUARY
Rocket	**SOW** after a year...					
Good King Henry						
Orache	**SOW**					
Spinach						
Mizuna greens						
Texcel greens		**SOW**				
Loose-leaved lettuce			**SOW**			
Pak choi						
Amaranthus						
Chrysanthemum greens						
American landcress						
Mibuna greens						
Lamb's lettuce						

KEY   Cut-and-come-again, sow more seed every week or two   Under crop covers

COMPANION PLANTING

Companion planting is something that has always been practised by gardeners but little researched by scientists. It is about how particular plants can benefit their neighbours. This can work in a series of ways:

✦ as a sacrificial crop for 'trap cropping'. The neighbour attracts the pest away from the main crop. Chinese cabbage gone to seed will attract aphids away from other cabbages.

✦ for symbiotic nitrogen fixing. The legumes – peas and beans – add nitrogen to the soil for the benefit of the neighbouring or subsequent crop.

✦ for biochemical pest suppression. Some plants exude chemicals that repel pests from their roots and leaves. The African marigold repels nematodes by exuding the chemical thiopene.

✦ by spatial interactions such as that provided by tall plants intercropped and shading smaller ones in the heat of summer – like lettuce under sweetcorn.

✦ by 'nurse cropping'. Windbreaks provided by vigorous tall plants such as Jerusalem artichokes to protect smaller, more vulnerable plants.

✦ by providing beneficial habitats. Plants are used to provide homes and nectar for beneficial predators.

Good neighbours

Although much more research is needed, trials have proved that growing carrots and leeks together reduces the levels of rust and thrips on the leeks and carrot fly on the carrots. Nasturtiums (and also the poached egg plant (*Limnanthes douglassii*) and marigolds of all sorts) increase the population of beneficial insects. Growing tomatoes with French marigolds has the effect of less whitefly and spider mite. Chives planted by roses results in reduced blackspot, while garlic deters aphids.

A monoculture of any particular type of plant is like putting up a giant hoarding advertising your plot as a sitting target to pests. When planning your allotment, think about biodiversity. Having lots of different types of plants, including flowers and herbs, will provide camouflage and will confuse and outwit the pests that go by sight and smell. The provision of suitable nectar plants, of habitats and water will draw in their predators. Aim for a well-balanced ecosystem. It is the best protection against pests that an organic gardener can have.

good idea

If you experience trouble with wireworms boring holes into your crops on a new plot, try sowing a row of wheat between them. The wireworms should home in on it and then you can dig up both wheat and worms and destroy them.

DID YOU KNOW?

Some plants contain a pest repellent. **Southernwood** (*artemisia arbrotanum*) was traditionally used tied into bundles to deter moths. A more acceptable mix for the wardrobe is lavender, rosemary and cotton lavender. They all exude essential oils that pests detest.

Wormwood (*artemisia vulgaris*) was known as the 'midge plant' for obvious reasons.

All the **marigold** family (*tagetes sp*) will put off nematodes and aphids. Not without reason is *tagetes minuta*, tall relative of the French marigold, nicknamed 'Stinking Roger'.

Onions, particularly garlic, have a strong sulphur smell that deters and confuses pests.

Mint puts off cabbage white larvae, aphids and flea beetles. Rats and mice don't care for it either.

Oregano deters cabbage butterflies.

CHAPTER

the
plans

The planting plans in this chapter are aimed to give a hint of the wide range of possibilities open to us. The Big Family Plot is the only plot shown in full through four seasons, while the others – with the exception of the labour-saving High-speed Plot – are shown as half plots. The idea is that in the other (unseen) half of the plot, there will be much the same standard produce, as well as the all-essential manure heap and compost bins.

THE BIG FAMILY PLOT

This is a traditional full-sized allotment used to maximum capacity all year round. Plans are given for all four seasons. The plants (listed on page 103) are tried and tested, are justifiably amongst the nation's favourites, and can be found in most catalogues. The allotmenteer of a big family plot will need to be a serious gardener, using plenty of crop covers to extend the season and maximize the crops. Most of the beds are the same width so that their cloches will fit anywhere and can be moved around allowing for maximum flexibility. In the old way, these plot holders manage well without a greenhouse or polytunnel by growing seed at home and having a good-sized nursery bed and two cold frames.

There are four rotation beds for potatoes, roots, legumes and brassicas. Onions and the beetroot family (including spinach) have their own quarters in the roots' bed and move around with them. They are good companions as all have a liking for free-draining sandy soil on the alkaline side. Near the shed are the perennial beds for artichokes, flowers for the house and culinary herbs. Raspberries and loganberries are grown against the boundaries by the shed. The autumn raspberries face south as they need full sun. Strawberries are moved to a new bed every third year. The central bed at the top end is a generous sized nursery bed and along with the cold frame, it is kept to a very high standard. Lettuce and other leafy salad crops are slotted where there is space. Carrots, radish and beetroot are grown successively right through the growing season with seed sown every two weeks. There are perennial beds for asparagus and rhubarb. A third bed is a useful extra space which will be used for sweetcorn this year.

The Big Family Plot: **SPRING**

In this plan shallots were started from sets during the winter and strong supports were put in ready for the loganberries and the summer raspberries. Along with the autumn raspberries they will arrive as 'rooted tips' in early spring. Strawberries grown from last year's runners are tidied up for the season ahead. Early carrots and leeks are started in the cold frame. At the end of April, second early carrots are sown *in situ*. Early turnips are started off in the cold frame. Later in the season they will be grown outside. Brussels sprouts, primo cabbage, sprouting broccoli and autumn cauliflowers are sown in the nursery bed. Broad beans and early peas are started where they are to grow under cloches. The chitted potatoes, first and second earlies and main crop, are planted around Easter, traditionally on Good Friday. Tomato, aubergine, outdoor cucumber, courgette and pepper plants are sown at home with heat or will be bought as young plants to go out at the end of May. The one-year-old asparagus crowns can be planted out in the specially prepared bed. They will be ready for harvesting in two years. Crowns of rhubarb planted in earliest spring will be ready in 15 months. The artichoke crowns are planted out along with perennial flowers and herbs.

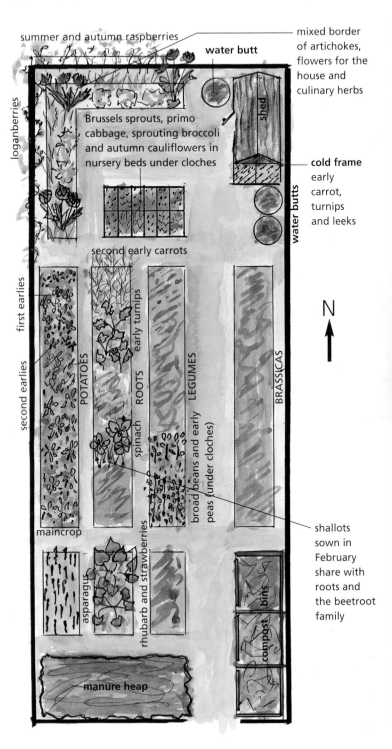

summer and autumn raspberries

water butt

mixed border of artichokes, flowers for the house and culinary herbs

loganberries

Brussels sprouts, primo cabbage, sprouting broccoli and autumn cauliflowers in nursery beds under cloches

shed

cold frame early carrot, turnips and leeks

water butts

second early carrots

first earlies

second earlies

POTATOES

early turnips

spinach

ROOTS

LEGUMES

broad beans and early peas (under cloches)

BRASSICAS

N

shallots sown in February share with roots and the beetroot family

maincrop

asparagus

rhubarb and strawberries

compost bins

manure heap

99

The Big Family Plot: **LATE SPRING, EARLY SUMMER**

Brussels sprouts, primo cabbage, sprouting broccoli, autumn cauliflowers and leeks raised in the nursery beds are planted out when large enough. Globe onion sets are planted out in late April. After all danger of frost has passed at the end of May, the French and runner beans are sown outside. In the South, sweetcorn can be sown in a block under cloches. In colder parts of the country it is wiser to start it under cover, or wait. In years to come this will be the time to enjoy fresh asparagus.

In June the new potatoes (first and second earlies) are harvested as and when needed as they don't store. The first broad beans, primo cabbage, carrots, early turnips and the early peas will be ready to eat by June as well as strawberries. The following year there will be loganberries and raspberries.

Once the danger of frost is over small plants of tomatoes, aubergines, peppers, cucumbers and courgettes that were raised at home go into nursery beds and cold frames.

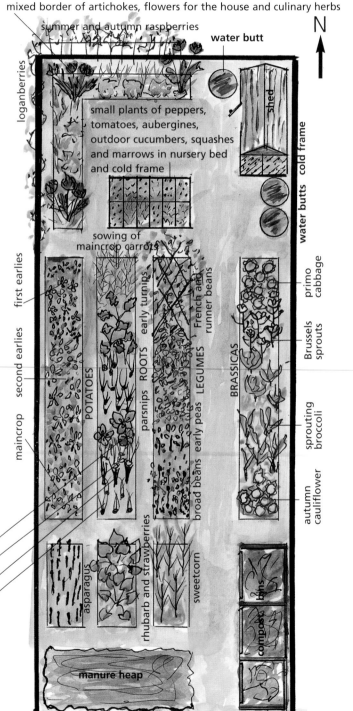

mixed border of artichokes, flowers for the house and culinary herbs

summer and autumn raspberries

water butt

loganberries

small plants of peppers, tomatoes, aubergines, outdoor cucumbers, squashes and marrows in nursery bed and cold frame

shed

cold frame

water butts

sowing of maincrop carrots

first earlies

second earlies

maincrop

POTATOES

parsnips

early turnips

ROOTS

French and runner beans

early peas

broad beans

LEGUMES

BRASSICAS

primo cabbage

Brussels sprouts

sprouting broccoli

autumn cauliflower

spinach

beetroot

leeks

globe onions

asparagus

rhubarb and strawberries

sweetcorn

bins

compost

manure heap

The Big Family Plot: **SUMMER**

From mid summer there is produce to be picked every day. The summer harvest includes French and runner beans, cabbage, cauliflowers, spinach, carrots, the last few peas, globe artichokes, beetroot, salad leaves, strawberries, summer raspberries and loganberries. The new potatoes (first and second earlies) and the peas are dug up and cleared away. The onions and shallots are lifted in July or August and left to dry in the sun.

There is now plenty of space for the tender fruiting vegetables. Tomatoes, peppers and aubergines belong to the potato family, so the potato bed is to be avoided. The cucurbits – cucumbers, marrows, squashes and courgettes can be slotted in wherever there is room, keeping in mind they need high fertility and plenty of water. They will keep fruiting until the frosts.

In August, the hottest month of year, it is time to start planning for winter. Spring cabbage, winter spinach, hardy peas, main crop carrots, winter leeks are sown in the nursery bed. Turnips for New Year's Eve are sown *in situ* as they dislike being moved.

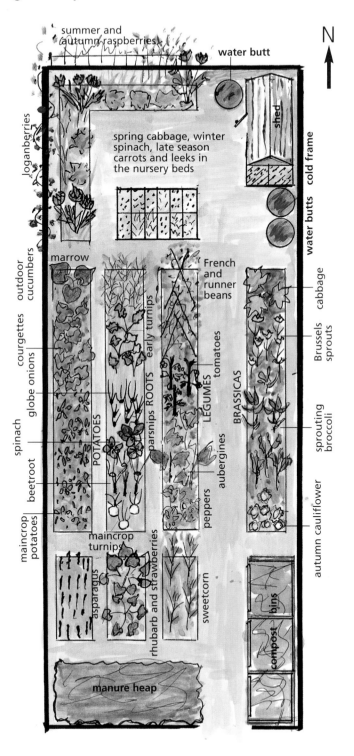

The Big Family Plot: **AUTUMN AND WINTER**

Before the frosts the maincrop potatoes, beetroot, carrots and summer turnips are lifted and stored.

Tomatoes, aubergines, peppers, cucumbers, courgettes, marrows, sweetcorn and autumn raspberries are consumed, bottled or frozen. Now there is room in the main beds for the parsnips, Brussels sprouts, spring cabbage, winter spinach and late season carrots. The salads are continued with hardy winter varieties grown under cloches in the nursery bed and cold frame.

Garlic, Japanese onion (or autumn-sown onion sets) and overwintering broad beans are sown in autumn. Green manures may be sown in the empty beds. Good types for winter are field beans, winter tare and rye grass. Other beds may be dug over to expose pests to the birds and to be broken down by the frosts.

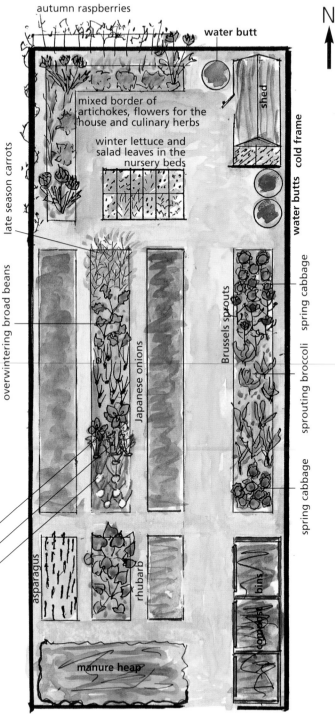

autumn raspberries

water butt

N

mixed border of artichokes, flowers for the house and culinary herbs

winter lettuce and salad leaves in the nursery beds

shed

cold frame

water butts

late season carrots

overwintering broad beans

Japanese onions

Brussels sprouts

spring cabbage

sprouting broccoli

spring cabbage

winter spinach

parsnips

maincrop turnips

asparagus

rhubarb

bins

compost

manure heap

Plant List for the Big Family Plot

BED ONE: Potatoes
First earlies
'Accent'
'Charlotte (salad potato)

Second earlies
'Maxine' or 'Nadine'

Maincrop
'King Edward'
'Sarpo Axona'

BED TWO: Roots and Onions
Carrots
'Amsterdam Forcing' or 'Early Nantes'
'Bangor' or 'Nantes 2'
'Autumn King'

Turnips
'Tokyo Cross'
'Golden Ball'

Parsnips
'Tender and True'

Shallots from sets
'Golden Gourmet'

Bulb onions from sets
'Ailsa Craig' or 'Centurion'

Japanese overwintering onion
'Senshyu Yellow'

Leeks
'King Richard' or 'Jolant'
'Musselburgh'
'Winter Crop'

BED THREE: Legumes
Broad beans
'Express'
'Aquadulce Claudia'

Peas
'Kelvedon Wonder'
'Show Perfection'

French beans
'The Prince'

Mangetout
'Oregon Sugar Pod'

Runner bean
'Scarlet Emperor'

BED FOUR: Brassicas
Brussels sprouts
'Pier Gynt' F1
'Noisette'

Summer cabbage
'Primo' or 'Greyhound'

Cauliflower
'Canberra'

Broccoli
'Early Purple Sprouting Improved'

Spring cabbage
'First Early Market'

Winter cabbage
'January King'or 'Celtic'

OTHERS
Aubergine
'Long Purple'
'Moneymaker'

Beetroot
'Bolthardy'
'Burpees Golden' or 'Bull's Blood'
'Detroit'

Courgette
'Defender'

Cucumber (outdoor)
'Burpless Tasty Green'

Loganberry
'LY654' (a thornless variety)

Peppers
'New Ace'
'Sweetcorn'
'Sundance'

Raspberries
'Glen Moy' (summer)
'Autumn Bliss' (autumn)

Spinach
'Atlanta'

Strawberries
'Cambridge Favourite'

Summer squash
'Patty Pan'

Tomatoes
'Gardener's Delight'
'Moneymaker'

THE HIGH-SPEED PLOT

The high-speed plot flies in the face of two fine allotment traditions – the art of relaxation and the culture of make do and mend. This plot has been prepared and organized over odd weekends through the winter. The aim has been to streamline it so that it won't take more than a couple of hours at the weekend plus three or four flying visits in the week to keep it in top condition. Time spent little but often is more effective than an occasional big onslaught.

This half plot has been organized into one-metre strips with narrow paths in between so that the plot holder can step over the beds at any point without treading on them. All the beds are raised (see page 133) with recycled boards and filled with top quality compost. The annual vegetables are grown under environmental mesh to cut out the majority of flying pests, rabbits, birds and the worst of the weather. As enviromesh doesn't look very attractive, these beds are hidden from view from the seat under a simple four-post pergola by a flowerbed spanning their width.

The plot is worked on the 'no dig' system (see page 132) thereby saving a lot of backbreaking work. Established plants are given a good mulch to keep in moisture to save on watering. To cut out weeding or mowing, the paths are made from recycled paving stones laid straight onto the soil

The plants are chosen for ease of culture, because they are remarkably delicious when home grown, or because they are expensive to buy in the shops. The perennials — asparagus, artichokes and rhubarb — are no trouble once planted and provide gourmet fare for years. Autumn raspberries are the most amenable of fruits. They produce in the first year and need no pruning apart from being cut right down in autumn.

Seed sowing is kept to a minimum. It is restricted to salad leaves, carrots, beetroot, radishes and some oriental *saladini* sown every two weeks through the growing season in a bed known as the 'Salad Bar'. The really rushed could buy their salad mixes on pre-sown biodegradable mats only needing to be laid on pots and watered. Most other vegetables are grown from plugs, crowns or sets rather than seed.

The Mediterranean plants — tomatoes, aubergines, courgettes and peppers — are bought as young plants and are grown on from June. Two or three plants of each are plenty for a small family so the cost is not great. Herbs are grown in half barrels in well-drained soil either from young plants or seed depending on type.

Most of the varieties chosen for this plot can be obtained as plug plants from the mainstream catalogues. Those with the RHS' Award of Garden Merit (AGM) are particularly favoured as they are virtually guaranteed to perform brilliantly.

The High Speed Plot: **SPRING AND EARLY SUMMER**

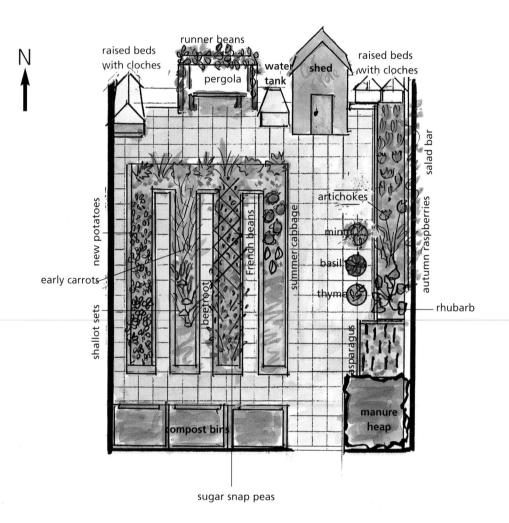

N

raised beds with cloches

runner beans

pergola

water tank

shed

raised beds with cloches

salad bar

new potatoes

early carrots

shallot sets

beetroot

French beans

summer cabbage

artichokes

mint

basil

thyme

asparagus

autumn raspberries

rhubarb

compost bins

manure heap

sugar snap peas

Here shallot sets, small plants of summer cabbage and sugar snap peas are planted out under cloches in March. The first early potatoes – a large red with good flavour and salad type – are chitted at home and planted out in mid-April. Rhubarb crowns, available in April, are generally dug up and moved every third year for maximum yield. In early May, artichoke, asparagus crowns and beetroot plugs are planted out. The 'Salad Bar' is started under cloches.

The High Speed Plot: **SUMMER AND AUTUMN**

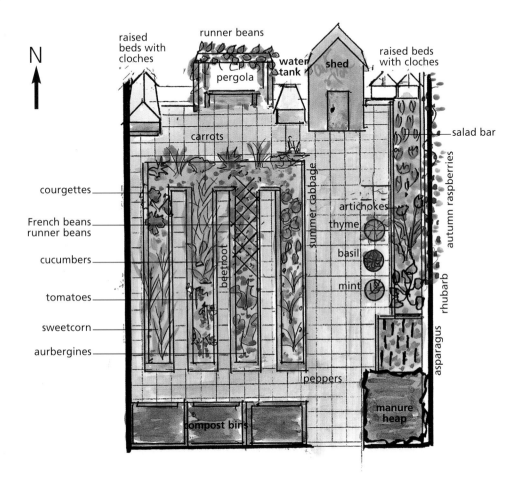

By the beginning of June the cabbages, carrots, beetroot and salad leaves are ready for harvest. The early potatoes and sugarsnap peas are cleared away. The young plants of outdoor cucumbers, French and runner beans, tomatoes, aubergines, sweetcorn and courgettes are planted out. They will be ready to harvest in July and August on a daily basis along with the autumn raspberries. This is not a winter plot, but in August collections of winter and oriental greens as well as salads are easy enough to plant out under cloches if required.

Plant List for the High-speed Plot

Artichoke
'Green Globe'
'Concerto' F1

Asparagus
'Connover's Colossal'
   (AGM)

Aubergine
'Bonica' F1 (AGM)

Beetroot
'Bolthardy'

Courgettes
'El Greco' (AGM)
'Patriot' F1

Dwarf French beans
'Cantare' (AGM)

Potato
'Red Duke of York' (AGM)
'Charlotte' (salad type)
   (AGM)

Rhubarb
'Victoria'

Runner Beans
'Enorma' (AGM)

Shallots
'Ambition'

Sugarsnap peas
'Delikett' (AGM)

Summer cabbage
'Duchy'
'Castello'

Tomato
'Alicante' (AGM)
'Sweet Million' (AGM)
'Gardener's Delight'
   (AGM)

THE ITALIAN PLOT

The idea of this allotment is to create a little Italy on a British allotment using Italian varieties wherever possible. The tomatoes, aubergines, peppers, courgettes, melon and beans are started off early at home in a heated propagator. The little polytunnel is useful for growing them on. To make a sheltered microclimate, Jerusalem artichokes (cultivated in Rome in the 17th century) make a 2 m (6 ft) windbreak on one side, while sweetcorn offers protection on the other in high summer.

Supposing this allotment is in the north of England, a grapevine would be unlikely to fruit well so a hop was chosen instead to climb up the trellis at the back. The young shoots will be used to make *risotto di bruscandoli* — a classic dish for *cucina povera* — the impoverished cook. Many Italian classics are merely different varieties of hardy vegetables commonly grown in the UK and can be sown straight out in the normal way.

A good selection of herbs is essential to Italian cuisine, as is a non-stop supply of 'bitter' leaves. The rosemary, lavender and thyme are particularly nostalgic and are placed to be brushed against in passing to release their aromatic scent. Everything is grown in narrow trenches in the old Italian way for water efficiency. In the half of the allotment not seen here, are the standard crops plus the manure and compost heaps.

The Italian Plot: **SPRING**

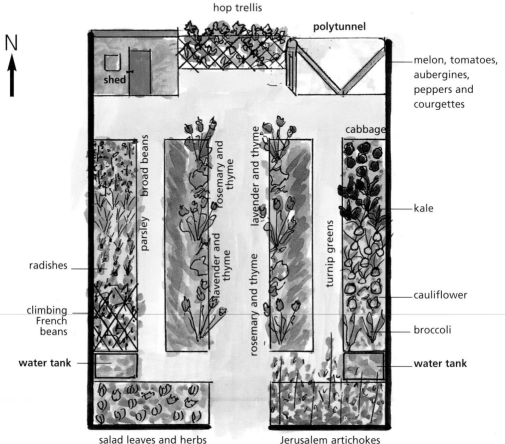

N
↑

hop trellis

polytunnel

shed

— melon, tomatoes, aubergines, peppers and courgettes

cabbage

parsley

broad beans

rosemary and thyme

lavender and thyme

lavender and thyme

rosemary and thyme

turnip greens

— kale

radishes —

climbing French beans —

water tank —

— cauliflower

— broccoli

— **water tank**

salad leaves and herbs

Jerusalem artichokes

From spring the tender vegetables – tomatoes, aubergines, courgettes, peppers and sweetcorn – can be propagated at home with heat, carefully hardened off and planted out in the polytunnel until summer. In the plot, Italian varieties of brassicas, the fava (or broad) beans and salad leaves are sown out under cloches in March and April. Florence fennel is sown *in situ* in May. The climbing French beans for drying are sown outside at the end of the month.

The Italian Plot: **SUMMER AND AUTUMN**

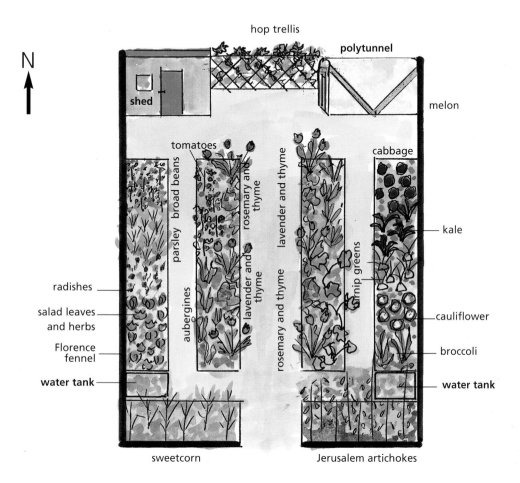

In high summer the tender vegetables and fruits are planted outside. The melon, being the most susceptible, luxuriates in the polytunnel. In August, sowings of winter spinach in the polytunnel will give the earliest crops for the following year. The salads, particularly the-cut-and-come-again types, will continue right through winter with successive sowings. Plotholders can get ahead with the very hardy broad bean 'Super Aquadulce' and a really hardy pea like 'Douce Provençe' or 'Kelvedon Wonder' for the earliest *risotto primavera* – a delicious way to celebrate the arrival of spring.

Plant List for the Italian Plot

Artichoke
'Violetto di Chioggia'

Aubergines
'Rosa Bianca'

Broad beans
'Witkeim Manita'
'Super Aquadulce'

Broccoli
'Romanesco'

Cabbage
'Cuor di Bue'

Cauliflower
'Verde Marchigiano'
'Sicilia Violetta'.

Courgettes
'Stiato di Napoli'
'Tondo di Piacenzo'
'Verde di Italia'.

Florence Fennel
'Zefo Fina'

French beans for climbing
'Viola Cornetti'

French beans for drying
'Barlotta Lingua di Fuoco'

Kale
'Nero di Toscano'

Melon
'Century' F1
'Sweetheart' F1

Peas
'Douce Provençe'
'Kelvedon Wonder'

Peppers
'Corno di Torro Rosso'

Radish
'Sicily Giant'

Salads
Lambs lettuce
Rocket
Corn salad 'Vit'
Sorrel
Radiccio 'Palla Rossa' or
   'Palla di Fuoco'
Cutting chicory
   'Biondissima di Trieste'
Frizzy endive 'Pancalieri'

Broad leaved endive
   'Scarola' or 'Misticanza'

Sweetcorn
'Ovation'

Tomato
'San Marzano'

Turnip greens
'Rapa Seca Testa'

Herbs
Basil 'Fine verde' or
   'Neapolitana'
Borage
Chives
Lavender 'Hidcote'
Mint
Marjoram
Oregano
Parsley 'Italian Giant'
Rosemary
Thyme

THE HERITAGE PLOT

Botanists and plant breeders are always striving to develop improved strains of vegetables and fruit whether it is by breeding in extra resistance to disease or greater productivity. Many old varieties get lost as they become less commercial and can only be found in heritage seed libraries. Other old varieties simply cannot be 'improved' and are widely available. In this plot every single plant is a golden oldie, most dating from the 19th century. The plot holders are exemplary in practising biodiversity. They put up plenty of bird boxes, feeders and insect hotels (made by binding hollow twigs together). More importantly, they may have a pond where frogs can breed and birds can drink and bathe. They plant lots of flowers in and around the vegetables specifically chosen to attract beneficial insects (see page 57). The odd parsnip and leek is left to flower. Around the pond they grow the marsh marigold (*Caltha*) for spring and the flag iris (*I. pseudocorus*) to provide cover for wildlife. They avoid planting vegetables in obvious blocks noticeable to pests. They are not too tidy in autumn, leaving stacks of twigs and piles of stones in odd corners where useful predators can take refuge.

The Heritage Plot: **SPRING AND EARLY SUMMER**

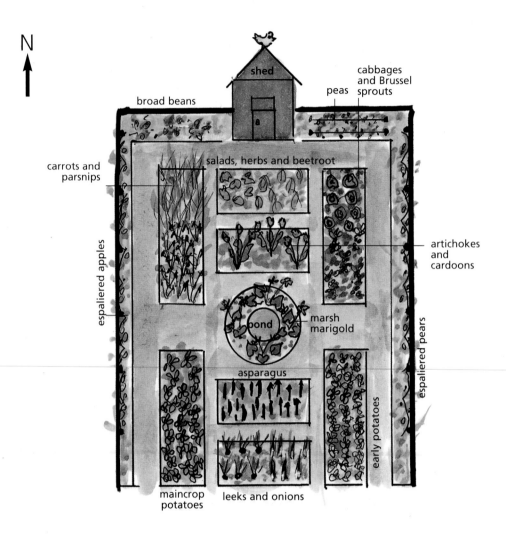

The very hardy broad bean 'Aquadulce' is sown out in February under cloches. First early and maincrop potatoes go in around Easter time. Carrots and peas are sown in early spring, as well as Brussels sprouts for Christmas eating. Leeks are sown out in mid-spring under cover. The rooted suckers of artichokes and cardoons (from neighbours or bought) are planted out. Parsnips from seed and onions from sets are started a few weeks later. 'January King' cabbages are sown in May for the following New Year. Runner and French beans can be sown outside at the end of the month on warmed soil with crop covers. Successional crops of salad leaves, carrots and beetroot are sown every two weeks from mid spring throughout the growing season. Asparagus from its third season onwards is harvested in May.

The Heritage Plot: **SUMMER ONWARDS...**

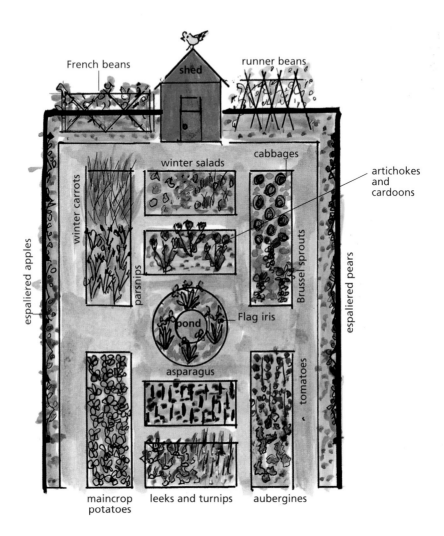

N

French beans

shed

runner beans

winter carrots

winter salads

cabbages

artichokes
and
cardoons

espaliered apples

parsnips

Brussel sprouts

espaliered pears

Flag iris

pond

tomatoes

asparagus

maincrop
potatoes

leeks and turnips

aubergines

By June it is time to lift the last of the early potatoes and clear away the peas. The tender vegetables – tomatoes and aubergines – can be planted out now in a sunny and sheltered spot. Covers can be taken off the French and runner beans. After the harvest in autumn, turnips are sown for spring greens and traditional salad greens are grown throughout winter under cloches.

Plant List for the Heritage Plot

Asparagus
'Connover's Colossal'
  (1873)

Aubergine
'Long Purple' (1830)

Beetroot
'Burpee's Golden' (1828)
'Bull's Blood' (C19th)

Broad bean
'Aquadulce' (1850)

Brussels sprouts
'Rubine' (1930s)

Cabbage
'January King' (1867)

Carrot
'Autumn King' (by 1900)
'Long Red Surrey' (1821)

French beans
'Blue Lake' (1885)

Leek
'Musselburgh' (1834)

Onion
'Ailsa Craig' (1887)

Parsnip
'Tender and True' (1897)

Potatoes
Earlies
'Duke of York' (1891)

Maincrop
'King Edward' (1910)

Salad potatoes
'Pink Fir Apple' (1850)
'Ratte' (1872)

Peas
'Alderman' (1890s)

Runner bean
'Painted Lady' (1633)

Salad leaves
'Webb's Wonderful'
  (1890)
'Little Gem' (1889)
'Winter Density' (C19th)
Chicory 'Witloof' (1850s)
Corn salad 'Verte de
  Cambrai' (C19th)

Salad onion
'Bedfordshire Champion'
  (1869)
'Dark Red Brunswick'
  (1870

Tomato
'Gardener's Delight'
  (C19th)
'Golden Queen' (1882)

Turnip
'Navet de Nancy' (1870)

Espaliered apples
'James Grieve'
'Cox's Orange Pippin'
(paired as pollinators for
  early autumn fruit)

Espaliered pears
'Doyenne de Comice'
'Glou Moreau'
(paired as pollinators for
  late autumn fruit)

THE ORNAMENTAL PLOT

This plot is designed to be as attractive as it is useful. The plot holder enjoys composing pictures out of the myriad shapes, forms, textures and colours to be found in the Vegetable Kingdom. In this particular year, the colour scheme for vegetables is hot by the hut with a theme of flaming reds and yellows that grade down to cool blues, violets and purples at the far end. Around the borders are the tall plants – sunflowers, angelicas, artichokes and sweetcorn. Tripods of French beans (yellow and purple) are underplanted with the bright Swiss chards. The central beds are planted in patterns. Not seen here, scorching orange nasturtiums at one end are offset by the cool azure of borage, hyssop, the little drumheads of chives. Green foliage is the link. Like the pictures in a kaleidoscope, the patterns are always changing as one crop is harvested and replaced by another. With this constant pattern movement it is easy to keep up the rotation.

The Ornamental Plot: **SPRING**

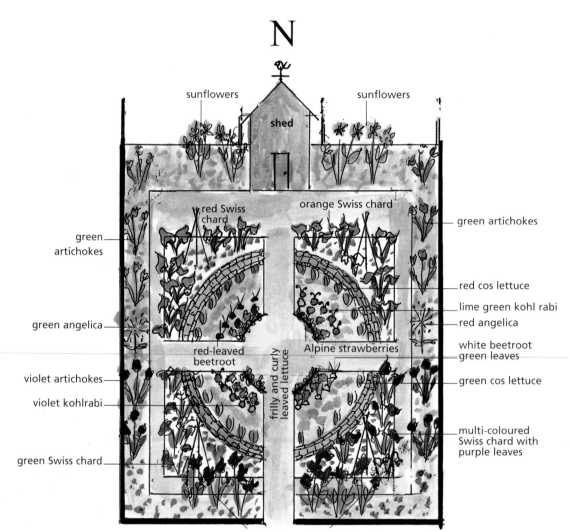

N

sunflowers

sunflowers

shed

green artichokes

red Swiss chard

orange Swiss chard

green artichokes

red cos lettuce

lime green kohl rabi

red angelica

green angelica

white beetroot green leaves

red-leaved beetroot

Alpine strawberries

frilly and curly leaved lettuce

green cos lettuce

violet artichokes

violet kohlrabi

multi-coloured Swiss chard with purple leaves

green Swiss chard

near black sunflowers

Swiss chard, beetroot, angelica, kohl rabi and lettuce are sown out under cloches and the artichoke offsets are planted April. Both golden and black sunflowers are sown in spring for a touch of theatre and to attract helpful insects. Some of the beds are edged with dainty alpine strawberries. The sweetcorn and outdoor cucumber seed are started at home.

The Ornamental Plot: **SUMMER**

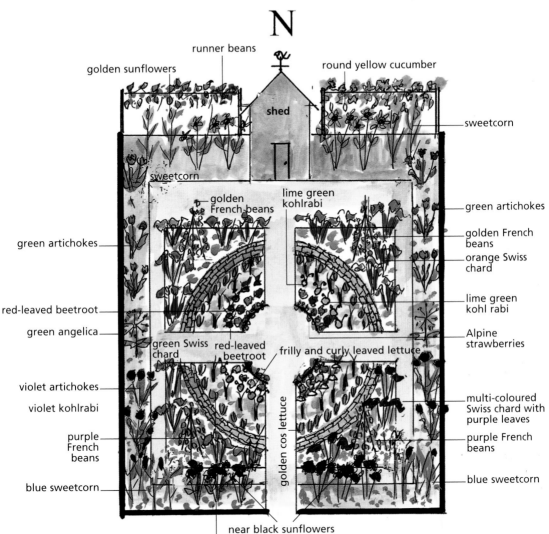

N

golden sunflowers

runner beans

round yellow cucumber

shed

sweetcorn

sweetcorn

golden
French beans

lime green
kohlrabi

green artichokes

green artichokes

golden French
beans

orange Swiss
chard

red-leaved beetroot

lime green
kohl rabi

green angelica

green Swiss
chard

red-leaved
beetroot

frilly and curly leaved lettuce

Alpine
strawberries

violet artichokes

violet kohlrabi

golden cos lettuce

multi-coloured
Swiss chard with
purple leaves

purple
French
beans

purple French
beans

blue sweetcorn

blue sweetcorn

green cos lettuce

near black sunflowers

In June the young plants of cucumber and sweetcorn can be planted outside. The French beans are sown *in situ*. Fast growers – different varieties of lettuce, salad leaves, kohlrabi, radishes and carrots – are sown wherever gaps appear. In August the highly decorative kales, 'Ragged Jack' 'Red Russian' and the 'Chou Palmier' (which is like a little palm tree) are started off from seed to replace the Swiss chard for winter impact. Next year the plan will include the dramatic foliage of rhubarb, and other decorative and curious vegetables – red orache with its graceful plumes, the feathery foliage of bronze fennel, giant black tomatoes, speckled aubergines the size of eggs, patty pan squash and striking cucurbits like the 'Turks' Turban' and the 'Crown of Thorns', edged with curly parsley and scented thymes.

Plant List for the Ornamental Plot

HOT COLOURS
Angelica
'Gigas'

Artichoke
'Green globe'

Beetroot
'Bulls Blood'

Cucumber
'Crystal Lemon'
Round yellow

French beans
'Corona d'Ora' or
  'Sungold'

Kohlrabi
'White Vienna'

Leeks
'Goliath'

Lettuce
'Red Salad Bowl'
'Lollo Verde'
'Red Cos'

Runner beans
'Scarlet Emperor'

Sunflower
'Giant Single'

Sweetcorn
'True Gold'

Swiss chard
'Ruby chard'
'Orange Fantasia'

COLD COLOURS
Artichoke
'Violette de Provençe'

Beetroot
'Albinia Verecunda'

French beans
'Blue Lake'
'Cosse Violette'
'Royalty'

Kohlrabi
'Purple Vienna'

Leeks
'Bleu Solaise'

Lettuce
'Salad Bowl'
'Oakleaf'
'Lobjoit's Green'

Sweetcorn
'Black Aztec'

Swiss chard
'Bright Lights'
'Fordhook Giant'

Sunflower
'Claret'

EDGING
Alpine strawberry
'Baron Sollemacher'

THE ORIENTAL PLOT

Over the past 15 years oriental vegetables, popular throughout China, Japan, Thailand and Vietnam, have been filtering through into British catalogues, causing an explosion of interest amongst gardeners. Some of the vegetables commonly used in oriental cuisine are subtropical and only thrive in the heated greenhouse in the UK, others just need the protection of the polytunnel or cloche through summer. In this plan the more tender species – okra, peppers, tomatoes, chillies, aubergines, amaranthus, melons, gourds, cucumbers and lemon grass – are tucked away in the polytunnel. The only calculated risk is the yard long bean that decorates the high south-facing fence.

The purpose of this plan is to concentrate on the oriental vegetables that are well adapted to the British climate and are grown outside. Oriental brassicas grow with speed and vigour and many can be used as cut-and-come-again for salads or stir fries when young, as small tender vegetables when semi-mature, or be grown through winter to maturity. A difference from the other plots is that the beds run east to west. They are high-ridged beds so that the south-facing side is on a sunny slope and the north-facing side is in shade. In high summer, the plants that like a little shade will be on the cool side and the sun loving ones on the sunny side. This is very much a working plot and no space is wasted. The beds are uniform grid of narrow strips for maximum efficiency.

The Oriental Plot: **SPRING**

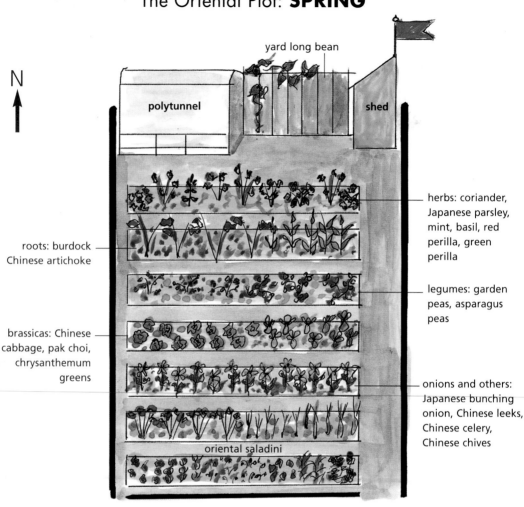

yard long bean

polytunnel

shed

N

herbs: coriander, Japanese parsley, mint, basil, red perilla, green perilla

roots: burdock Chinese artichoke

legumes: garden peas, asparagus peas

brassicas: Chinese cabbage, pak choi, chrysanthemum greens

onions and others: Japanese bunching onion, Chinese leeks, Chinese celery, Chinese chives

oriental saladini

In spring herbs are planted out in *situ* under cloches. Burdock seed is sown in earliest spring as well as the tubers of the Chinese artichoke, prized for their jade-like roots. Being a relative of mint they are not really in the 'roots' category, any more than the radishes that follow them, but they like the same style of soil – rich, sandy and free-draining. Summer legumes include pea shoots – ordinary peas harvested after a month for their delicious tender shoots. The asparagus pea with its red pea flowers and winged pods is another rare delicacy. Sow in May and harvest when the pods are about 2.5 cm (1 in) long. From the vast array of oriental brassicas, you can grow loose-headed cabbage, pak choi and chop suey greens – the edible chrysanthemum. Raise the biennial Chinese chives in the polytunnel and transplant out in spring to join the oriental bunching onions and some Chinese celery sown out in April. One bed is entirely devoted to CCA 'oriental saladini'. It is divided into three and fresh seed sown every two weeks through summer.

The Oriental Plot: **AUTUMN AND WINTER**

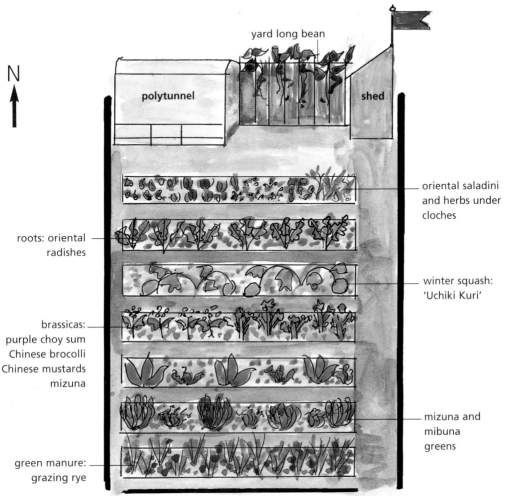

yard long bean

N

polytunnel

shed

oriental saladini
and herbs under
cloches

roots: oriental
radishes

winter squash:
'Uchiki Kuri'

brassicas:
purple choy sum
Chinese brocolli
Chinese mustards
mizuna

mizuna and
mibuna
greens

green manure:
grazing rye

In midsummer there is a second wave of sowing and planting for autumn and winter. The seed of giant oriental radishes will take about three months to mature and will enjoy the nip of autumn. As the burdock is harvested in autumn the giant radishes can go in. The Chinese artichokes will be ready to harvest by early winter. As the peas finish in midsummer, the winter squashes that have been raised inside are given room to sprawl in their own bed. Chinese broccoli sown in summer will give a fine autumn harvest. Purple choy sum, grown for its flowering shoots, is best sown in August outside for harvesting in early winter. A further sowing can be made in late autumn to last through the winter in the polytunnel. This the best time to sow mizuna and mibuna greens. The broad-leaved mustards are very hardy and are sown between August and October to last throughout till spring. As beds empty green manures are sown to keep the plot in good order until spring.

Plant List for the Oriental Plot

Herbs
Coriander 'Cilantro' for
  leaves and 'Moroccan'
  for seeds
Japanese parsley
  'Mitsuba'
Mint
Basil *Horophu Rau Que*,
  'Sacred Kha Prao' and
  'Siam Queen'
Red perilla
Green perilla

Roots
Burdock 'Watanabe Early'
Chinese artichoke
Radish 'Minowasi
  Summer' F1 and 'April
  Cross'

Legumes
Garden peas
Asparagus pea

Brassicas
Pak Choi 'Joy Choi' F1
Loose-headed Chinese
  cabbage 'Maruba
  Santo'
Chrysanthemum greens
  'Shungiko'
Chinese broccoli 'Green
  Lance'
Chinese mustard 'Red
  Giant' and 'Green in the
  Snow'
Mizuna 'Green Spray'
Mibuna 'Tokyo Beau'

Onions
Japanese bunching onion
  'Yoshima' and 'Long
  White Koshigaya'
Chinese leek/garlic chives
Chinese celery 'Kintsai'
Oriental saladini
Winter squash 'Uchiki
  Kuri'

Green manure
Grazing rye

THE CARIBBEAN PLOT

The multi-cultural cuisine of the Caribbean islands is based on its famous tropical vegetation – papayas, mangoes, breadfruit, coconuts, plantains, avocados and other exotic fruits along with the black eyed peas and lima beans that grow wild. While most of these are difficult to grow (to say the least) in the UK allotment without heat and special conditions, it is amazing what can be done. The idea behind this plot is to push back the boundaries of growing exotic produce in a temperate climate. There are undoubtedly risks attached. However, seed merchants have been working to create hardier varieties or ones that mature faster in our shorter summers. The tropical sweet potato can now be purchased half grown to give it a head start. Most of the seed sowing is done at home with heated propagators or young plants are bought ready to go out. Extensive cold frames are installed to harden off young plants and to grow on the most tender ones. Given a sheltered sunny spot in the south of the UK, the rest of the vegetables are fine outside from June. In the north they may need cover.

The Caribbean Plot: **SUMMER**

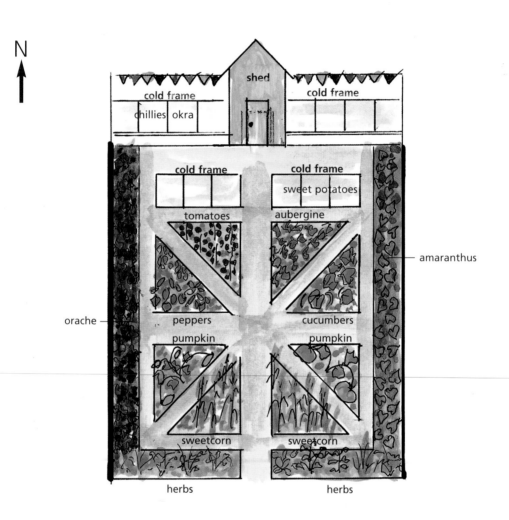

N

One of the plants most sensitive to cold is okra, a key ingredient of the Creole cuisine so popular in the Caribbean. Okra needs to be sown six weeks before the end of frosts and kept at 24°C (75°F). Peppers need to be eight to eleven weeks old before they can go out in the garden in mid-summer. Both should be watered with warm water. Sweet potatoes need five months to grow at an ideal temperature of 20–30°C (68–86°F). By June, the young plants of outdoor cucumbers, tomatoes, aubergine, sweetcorn, pumpkins, peppers and chillis are hardened off ready to go out. The decorative leaf amaranthus, better known as 'Love-lies-a-bleeding' or 'calaloo', is sown under cover or in hot summers, outside. Red orache (red mountain spinach) is sown every two or three weeks as it is likely to go to seed in mid-summer. Fenugreek, grown as much for the leaves as the seeds in the Caribbean, is be sown out in spring along with many herbs.

The Caribbean Plot: **AUTUMN ONWARDS...**

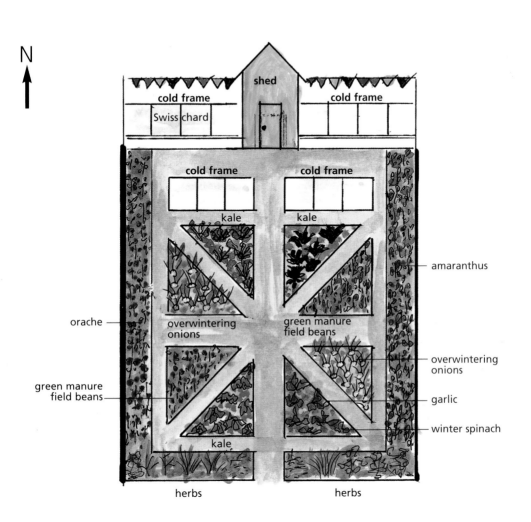

After the harvest you will need hardy European substitutes to carry you through the winter. Good winter greens to go with salt fish include the kales. These are sown in late spring, transplanted in July and will be ready from November onwards. Winter spinach is sown in August or September for early spring. The Swiss chards are sown in late summer and over-wintered in the cold frames for spring eating. Over-wintering onions and garlic are planted out for the following summer. Cloches are put over the herbs to extend the season. In the empty beds, the field bean (*Vicia faba*) is sown as a green manure. It will make a good mulch when dug in next spring as well as adding nitrogen to the soil to benefit the next lot of brassicas.

Plant List for the Carribean Plot

Amaranthus

Aubergine
'Long Tom'
'Sweetcorn'

Chard
'Bright Lights'

Chilli peppers
'Early green Jalapeno'

Cucumbers
'West Indian Gherkin'
'Bush Champion' F1

Garlic

Kale
'Red Russian'
'Winterbor'
'Nero di Toscana'

Orache (red)
'Opera'

Okra
'Clemson Spineless' (half hardy)

Onions
'White Lisbon Winter Hardy'

Pumpkin
'Blue Banana'
'Connecticutt Field'

Spinach
'Giant Winter'

Sweetcorn
'Early Extra Sweet' F1
'Earlybird'

Sweet pepper
'Yankee Bell'
'Lipstick'

Sweet potato

Tomatoes
'San Marzano'

CHAPTER

6

glossary
of
techniques

PREPARING THE GROUND

Autumn is the best time to dig heavy soils. If they are left roughly turned over, the frosts will break them down further and the birds will demolish any soil-borne pests brought to the surface. Early spring is the best time to dig light soils as winter rain can 'leach', or wash away, the nutrients.

Single digging

Topsoil is excavated down to the level of one 'spit' – (spade length). This will give you the opportunity to pick out the roots of perennial weeds and to enrich the soil with compost and manure as you go.

The classic method is to mark out your space with pegs and string. Dig one spit deep into the first trench removing the topsoil and laying it on one side. Break up the subsoil beneath if necessary by stabbing it with a fork. Dig up the second spit in the same way, remove any weed roots, mix in some manure or compost into the top soil and put it into the hole left by the first spit. Work your way up and down in strips ending up by putting the soil from the first spit into the last hole.

SINGLE DIGGING

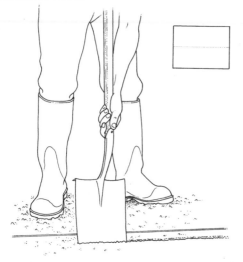

1 Mark out the area to be dug with a line.

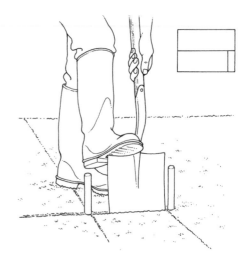

2 Dig the first trench one spit deep.

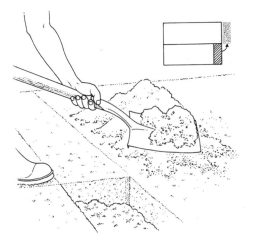

3 Lay the excavated topsoil on one side.

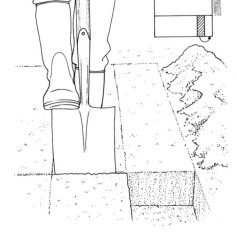

4 Dig a parallel trench.

5 Put the soil from the second trench into the first one, incorporating well-rotted manure or compost.

6 Carry on down the line finally adding the first pile of soil into the last trench.

Double digging

Helpful where there is poor drainage due to compacted subsoil. It is vital to keep the fertile topsoil and the infertile subsoil separate and to put them back in their correct layers. The method is to dig a trench one spit deep and two spades wide to remove the topsoil. This is barrowed to where you plan to end digging and left on one side. The first trench is then dug again to the depth of another spit and the subsoil is taken to where you are going to end up – but kept separate from the pile of topsoil. Then the subsoil from the second half of the trench is dug up and tipped into the first trench. The topsoil from the third strip is mixed with organic matter and put on top and so on down the line ending up by adding the piles of subsoil and then the topsoil that you started with into the last trench.

No digging

Too much digging can damage the soil structure and upset the delicate chemical balance. Once you have good drainage and have dealt with the perennial weeds, the no dig system can work extremely well with the added benefit of saving your back. To work it's vital that the beds are never be walked on and compacted, so they are made

CREATING RAISED BEDS

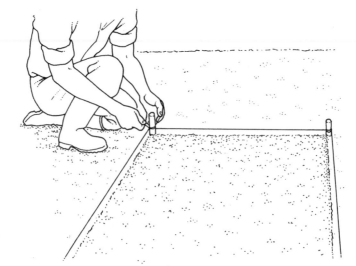

1 Mark out the space with pegs and string.

narrow enough to be cultivated from all sides. They are kept covered by crops, green manures or mulches, at all times to avoid any compaction or leaching from heavy rain. The policy is minimum disturbance and maximum layering on of good organic material. Seed is sown into this top layer – even potatoes are grown on top in straw and mulch. With the additional rich organic matter being piled on, the worm population burgeons. They will do the 'digging' for you, making air channels and improving the structure. Another benefit is that weed seed will not be brought to the surface to germinate.

Raised beds

Raised beds save time and labour. They keep paths and beds separate and your carefully worked fertile soil and organic matter in the right place and nowhere else. They warm up quickly in spring and you can control the drainage and the type of soil if you import the particular compost that you want. The height can vary according your needs and almost any edging – stones, bricks, logs sawn in half or old tiles will do the trick. If you can get hold of old planks, a neat edging can be made quite easily.

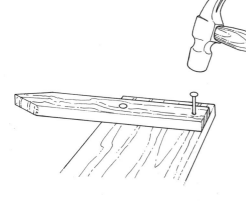

2 Nail short battens with pointed ends onto wooden planks.

3 Tap the pegs with the plank attached into the ground.

SOWING SEED OUTSIDE

Prepare the beds carefully. Once cleared of weeds and stones, the soil should be worked to a fine 'tilth'. The finer the seed, the finer the tilth. Aim for the texture of breadcrumbs by patiently moving the rake backwards and forwards over the bed, first in one direction and then another. Then smooth and slightly consolidate the ground with the back of the rake.

Drills

Generally vegetable seed is sown in straight lines or a geometric pattern to help the gardener discern which seedling is which. Use pegs and string to get straight lines and make a drill with the corner of a hoe or a stick (see opposite). Be careful not to make it too deep. Sow the seed by holding it in the palm of one hand and taking pinches with the other or by rubbing it through finger and thumb. Fine seed can be mixed with silver sand or sieved dry soil to make it easier to distribute it sparingly. Finish off by tapping a dusting of fine compost through a sieve over the seeds.

Station sowing

Large seeds – beans and peas – are sown individually. A measuring stick is useful for marking off the planting distances. Make a hole with a dibber and drop the seeds in one by one. It is customary to sow three seeds per station and thin to one later.

Broadcasting seed

The broadcasting method is used for a carpet covering, like lawn or small-seeded green manures. This is done by walking up and down the area to be covered and scattering seed in a wide arc of the arm. Avoid windy days.

Fluid sowing

Fluid sowing is a commercial technique aimed to give seeds a head start. It can easily be adapted to home use and it is excellent for erratic seed like that of parsnip and carrot, or to speed up the growing process of any seed. The seeds are pre-germinated, dropped into a 'carrier gel' and squeezed out into the soil. To pre-germinate, put the seeds on wet kitchen towel in a plastic container, cover them with a plastic bag and put them in a dark warm place like the airing cupboard. Watch them carefully over the next few days. You want to catch them when still embryonic with almost invisible tiny roots just coming through. Rinse them carefully off the kitchen towel. Make up a mixture of the water-retaining granules sold in garden centres. Drop in a few seeds with the tip of a plant label or tweezers. If they sink the paste needs to be thicker. When you are satisfied, cut the corner off a heavy weight plastic bag and squeeze out the seeds into the prepared drill rather as if you were icing a giant cake. Cover with compost and keep well watered.

Making a drill with the corner of a hoe.

Sowing seed by rubbing it through finger and thumb.

Thinning

Thinning seeds is essential to give plants the best possible chance to realise their potential. Check on planting distances to get the optimum distance and be ruthless. Sometimes, the thinnings can be transplanted (or eaten, like carrots).

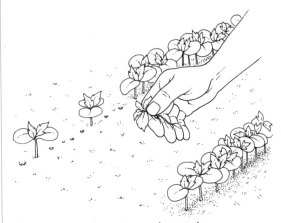

Thinning to get the optimum planting distances.

TRANSPLANTING

To minimize transplanting shock, prepare the bed first and make planting holes. Water both the soil and your seedlings well before attempting to move them. Wait for the cool of evening. Then work quickly and efficiently. Roots of young seedlings dry out in minutes when out of the soil. If you have to handle the plant pick it up by the leaves, not the delicate stem.

Always take as much soil as possible with the transplants. Better still is to grow your seedling in root trainers or biodegradable flowerpots. Plant to the same level as they were in their pots or seed trays. The one exception to this rule is leeks. These are dropped into deeper pre-prepared holes to keep them blanched.

TRANSPLANTING

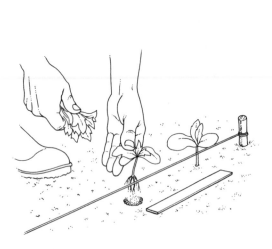

When transplanting or planting out always use a measuring stick and line so that your rows are straight and the plants are evenly spaced.

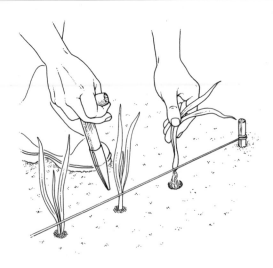

Young leeks are dropped into pre-prepared holes to a deeper level than before to blanche them, using a dibber.

For plants with a large root system, make a wider hole so that the roots can spread. Firm the soil back in around the plant carefully.

Keep the plants well watered until the transplants establish.

In the heat of summer, a little shading can easily be rigged up with sticks and newspaper.

Once the plants are established, continue to water and surround with a layer of organic mulch. This will prevent water loss from the roots.

PROTECTING YOUR CROPS

Cloches

The cloche is designed to be moved from one bed to the next to provide shelter and warmth where needed. If your cloches are of a standard size that will fit over your standard sized beds you will have maximum flexibility. Cloches come in glass, clear rigid plastics or heavy polythene. Large plastic water bottles with the bottom sawn off and the top left off for air circulation works well for individual plants. Other options are the mini polytunnels. These are easily made with wire hoops and heavy gauge clear polythene. Runner beans are vigorous self-clinging climbers that need strong supports at least 2.4 m (8 ft) tall. First introduced to Britain as ornamentals, runner beans look decorative on wigwams or over arches. They can also be grown up strings. The most practical support, however, is a row of criss-cross poles, tied where they cross and secured further with a horizontal pole across the top.

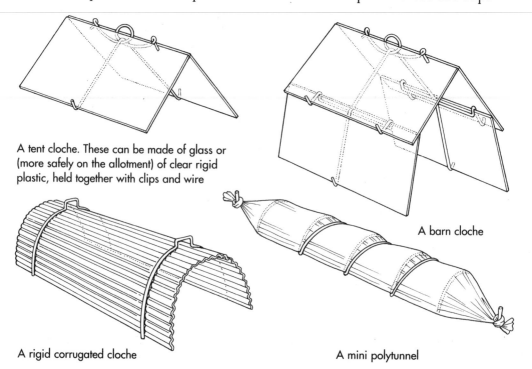

A tent cloche. These can be made of glass or (more safely on the allotment) of clear rigid plastic, held together with clips and wire

A barn cloche

A rigid corrugated cloche

A mini polytunnel

The cold frame

This is invaluable for raising
seedlings, hardening off young
crops, growing on tender ones and
for extending the season. It is
simply a box usually on the tilt to
catch the sun, with a removable lid
for ventilation and to prevent crops
getting scorched in hot weather.

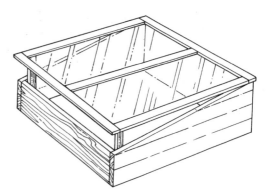

A cold frame with a hinged lid

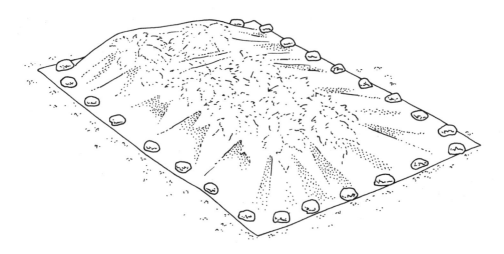

A crop grown under a floating mulch.

Fleece and mesh

Horticultural fleece and the more
resilient enviromesh netting have
transformed the lives of organic
gardeners. They keep out all
flying pests as well as rabbits and
mice. They give some protection
against the weather while letting
in moisture, air and light. Used
as a 'floating mulch', crops can be
grown completely encased by
them throughout their growth.
The mesh is usually buried at the
edges and held down with stones
or bricks with enough slackness
to allow for growth. Alternatively
they can be draped over a wire
frame and secured as above.

PLANT SUPPORTS

Runner beans are vigorous self-clinging climbers that need strong supports at least 2.4 m (8 ft) tall. Raspberries and other climbing fruits will also need support.

Bean supports The most practical support is a row of criss-cross poles, tied where they cross and secured further with a horizontal pole across the top.In windy areas, you can reinforce your bean supports by driving a stake alongside one or two corner canes and tying firmly.

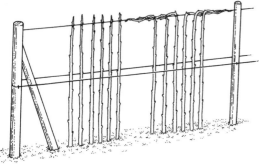

Training summer raspberries
In the hedgerow system the old canes are cut out after fruiting. The new canes are trained through the double wires and trimmed off in spring at the top of the wire or bent over and tied in.

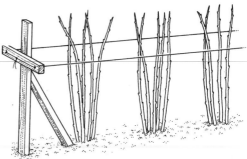

Free standing supports
In allotments there is rarely a fence or wall to train soft fruit and a free standing arrangement with cross posts and double wires makes a satisfactory support for growing the cane fruits.

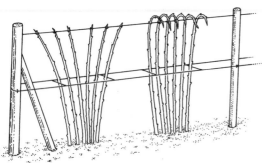

Training blackberries and hybrids – the stool system.
After fruiting, cut the plant down to the ground to leave half a dozen healthy new canes. Spread these out into a fan shape to catch the sun and for air circulation and tie them in. Either trim off at the top of the wire or bend them over.

140

SUPPLIERS AND USEFUL ADDRESSES

ORGANIZATIONS

The Allotment Regeneration Initiative
The Green House
Hereford Street, Bedminster
Bristol BS3 4NA
Tel: 0117 963 1551
www.farmgarden.org.uk

Community Composting Network
67 Alexandra Road
Sheffield S2 3EE
Tel: 0114 258 0483
www.othas.org.uk/ccn/

COSI (Centre for Organic Food Information)
www.cosi.org.uk.
COSI is run by the Soil Association and NIAB (The National Institute for Agricultural Botany) and supported by DEFRA (see below). It also co-operates with Garden Organic to trial different vegetables for disease resistance. The results are available on their website.

Department for the Environment, Food and Rural Affairs (DEFRA)
Nobel House
17 Smith Square
London SW1P 3JR
Tel: 020 7238 6000
www.defra.gov.uk

Federation of City Farms and Community Gardens
The Greenhouse
Hereford Street
Bristol BS3 4NA
Tel: 0117 923 0483
www.farmgarden.org.uk

Garden Organic
Ryton Organic Gardens
Coventry CV8 3LG
Tel: 024 7630 3517
www.gardenorganic.org.uk
Formerly the Henry Doubleday Research Association (HDRA). Offers open gardens, a magazine, events and an opportunity to join the Heritage Seed Library. Advice line for members. For seeds see Chase Organics.

National Allotments Week
Neil Dixon
12 Flamstead Crescent
King's Tamerton, Plymouth
Devon PL5 2AX
Tel: 01752 363379
www.nsalg.org.uk

National Society of Allotment and Leisure Gardeners
O'Dell House, Hunter's Road
Corby, Northants NN17 5JE
Tel: 01536 266576
www.nsalg.org.uk

Qed The Virtual Potting Shed
www.btinternet.com/~richard.
wiltshire/potshed1.htm
Very active site, useful for keeping your finger on the pulse of allotment politics and more.

Soil Association
Bristol House
40-56 Victoria Street
Bristol BS1 6BY
Tel: 0117 914 2400
www.soilassociation.org
At the heart of organic farming. Good website for catching up on issues.

SEED MERCHANTS

Association Kokopelli
Ripple Farm, Crundale
Canterbury, Kent CT4 7EB
Tel: 01227 731815
www.terredesemences.com
Started in France, they offer a wide ranging selection of unusual and heritage organic seed. Informative, well-written catalogue with interesting snippets of history and growing tips.

Jennifer Birch
Garfield Villa, Belleview Road
Stroud, Glos. GL5 2BS
Tel: 01453 750371
Supplies named varieties of French garlic.

Chase Organics
Order line: 0845 130 1304
www.OrganicCatalogue.com
The official mail order catalogue for Garden Organic, Chase Organics has a wide selection of organic seed, including seed from Seeds of Change (USA), Rijk Zwaan (Netherlands) and Ferme de St. Marthe (France).

Chiltern Seeds
Bortree Stile, Ulverston
Cumbria, LA12 7PB
Tel: 01229 581137
www.chilternseeds.co.uk
Good list of vegetables, including oriental ones and interesting varieties.

Delfland Nurseries Ltd
Benwick Road
Doddington, March
Cambridgeshire PE15 0TU
Tel: 01354 740553
www.organicplants.co.uk
Suppliers of organic vegetable
plug plants.

Dobies
Long Road, Paignton
Devon TQ4 7SX
Tel: 0870 1123625
www.dobies.co.uk
Good choice of 'pot ready'
plants.

Thomas Etty & Son
45 Forde Aveneue, Bromley
Kent BR1 3EU
Tel: 020 8466 6785
Small firm providing heritage,
unusual and regional varieties.

Mr Fothergill's Seeds
Gazeley Road, Kentford
Suffolk CB8 7QB
Tel: 0845 1662511
www.mr-fothergills.co.uk
Good selection of heritage,
organic, oriental, show bench.

The Green Chronicle
www.greenchronicle.co.uk
Online organic vegetable
seeds.

Kings Seeds
Monks Farm, Coggeshall
Road, Kelveden
Essex CO5 9PG
Tel: 01376 570000
www.kingsseeds.com
Largest supplier of seed for
the amateur grower in the
UK. Household name.
Official supplier for the
National Society of Allotment
and Leisure Gardeners.

Peppers By Post
Sea Spring Farm
West Bexington, Dorchester
Dorset DT2 9DD
Tel: 01308 897766
www.peppersbypost.biz

The Real Seed Catalogue
Brithdir Mawr, Newport
Pembrokeshire SA42 OQJ
Tel: 01239 821 107
www.realseeds.co.uk
Specialises in Mediterranean
varieties adapted to cooler
climates.

Seeds By Size
45 Crouchfield
Hemel Hempstead
Hertfordshire HP1 1PA
www.seeds-by-size.co.uk
A gene bank started by one-
man enthusiast, John Robert
in 1979. Over 8,000 varieties
of vegetable, herb and flower
seed. Can be purchased in
any quantity.

Simpson's Seeds
The Walled Garden Nursery
Horningsham, Warminster
Wiltshire BA12 7NQ
Tel: 01985 845004
www.simpsonsseeds.co.uk
Strong on exotics –
capsicums, aubergines etc.

Suffolk Herbs
Monk's Farm
Coggeshall Road, Kelvedon
Essex CO5 9PG
Tel: 01376 572456
www.suffolkherbs.com
Supplies a good range of
organic herbs and interesting
vegetables.

Suttons
Woodview Road, Paignton
Devon TQ4 TNG
Tel: 0870 220 2899
www.suttons-seeds.co.uk

Established firm since 1806.
Has the 'Alan Titchmarsh'
collection of organic vegetables. Good line in 'pot
readies' and AGM plants.

Tamar Organics
Tavistock Woodlands Estate
Gulworthy, Tavistock
Devon PL19 8JE
Tel: 01822 834690
Specializes in organic prod-
ucts. Wide range, including
orientals and green manures.

Thompson & Morgan
Poplar Lane, Ipswich
Suffolk 1P8 3BU
Tel: 01473 688821
www.thompson-morgan.com
International company. Good
choice in vegetables including
collections of seed, unusual
and new varieties. Specializes
in 'plugs'.

Edwin Tucker & Sons
Brewery Meadow, Stonepark
Ashburton, Devon TQ13
7DG
Tel: 01364 652233
www.edwinbtucker.com
Established in 1831. Broad
selection of old and new.

Unwins
Unwins Seeds Ltd Mail Order
Freepost ANG10815,
Wisbech
Cambridgeshire PE13 2BR
Tel: 01945 588522
www.unwins-seeds.co.uk
Old and new vegetables,
including the asparagus pea
and Chinese aubergines.

Vida Verde
14 Southdown Avenue
Lewes, East Sussex BN7 1EL
www.vidaverde.co.uk
Unusual varieties.

INDEX